MAPS FOR A FIESTA

MAPS FOR A FIESTA

A Latina/o Perspective on Knowledge
and the Global Crisis

OTTO MADURO

EDITED AND WITH AN INTRODUCTION
BY EDUARDO MENDIETA

FORDHAM UNIVERSITY PRESS ❖ NEW YORK ❖ 2015

Maps for a Fiesta: A Latina/o Perspective on Knowledge and the Global Crisis was previously published by Asociación para la Educación Teológica Hispana as *Mapas para la Fiesta: Reflexiones sobre la crisis y el conocimiento*, copyright © 1999 Otto Maduro.

Fordham University Press has no responsibility for the persistence or accuracy of URLs for external or third-party Internet websites referred to in this publication and does not guarantee that any content on such websites is, or will remain, accurate or appropriate.

Fordham University Press also publishes its books in a variety of electronic formats. Some content that appears in print may not be available in electronic books.

Visit us online at www.fordhampress.com.

Library of Congress Cataloging-in-Publication Data

Maduro, Otto, 1945–2013.
  [Mapas para la fiesta. English]
  Maps for a fiesta : a latina/o perspective on knowledge and the global crisis / Otto Maduro ; edited and with an Introduction by Eduardo Mendieta. — First edition.
    pages cm
  Includes bibliographical references and index.
  ISBN 978-0-8232-6304-2 (cloth : alk. paper) — ISBN 978-0-8232-6305-9 (pbk. : alk. paper)
    1. Knowledge, Theory of.   2. Reason.   3. Philosophy, Latin American.
  I. Mendieta, Eduardo, editor.   II. Title.
  BD165.M26313 2015
  121—dc23

                                                                      2014047803

Printed in the United States of America
17 16 15   5 4 3 2 1
First edition

CONTENTS

INTRODUCTION TO THE ENGLISH-LANGUAGE EDITION: TOWARD AN EPISTEMOLOGY OF LIBERATION

This book was meant to include a foreword to the first English edition, by Otto Maduro, but he passed away on May 9, 2013, before he could finish the manuscript. Otto Maduro was surely one of the best-known Latino theologians in the United States.[1] He was active within the academia, the churches, and community organizations, advocating, funding, and directing many initiatives on behalf of Latina/o priests, pastors, religious workers, community activists, and of course, students. He was also actively engaged in the Latina/o immigrant communities of New Jersey. He was an institution builder, a generous and engaged mentor. Wherever he went, he left an indelible memory. The numerous testimonials that have been given about him attest to his ebullient, larger-than-life, welcoming, jovial, and community-making personality. This book had a special significance for him. It was written in Spanish, and it was based on decades of social work and activism in the poor neighborhoods, prisons, and hospitals of Caracas, Venezuela, his birth city. The book went through two other editions and revisions, in Spanish. Before his death, Otto had been, with the help of Martha Swann, translating, editing, revising, and expanding the original text, to include his last two decades of teaching and mentoring in the United States. It is my honor to see this manuscript to its publication, after Helen Tartar saw that Fordham University Press would publish it. It is tremendously saddening to me that neither will see it in print.

As with the original Spanish edition, the book has a distinct format. This is no scholarly treatise, although it is full of wisdom and disarmingly articulated critiques and insights. The book could not, in fact, be an academic *tractatus*, for it would contradict one of its most important claims, namely that while ignorance is masked in the language of expertise, true knowledge is dismissed because it is sometimes articulated by so-called noncredible epistemic agents in pedestrian and demystifying language. It must be asked, nonetheless, what is the genre in which this book is written? And does this genre detract or augment the value of its content? It is in fact not an academic book, per se. But it is not "fiction." Is it autobiography? Partly, but it is more. Is it a series of lectures? No, certainly not, but the voice of the author is always present, clear, inviting, generous, solicitous. Is it about theology? Partly, and yet is also more. Is it like an extended letter to old friends? It does sometimes read like a long letter, full of personal and philosophical reflections. Is it a memoir? No, it is more like the trace of an intellectual itinerary. It is an amorphous, heterodox, and unsuspecting text in this age of hyperspecialized, über-arcane, and etherealized academese. Its virtues, however, are many. When I first read the book, I could not put it down. I felt like I was having a good old friend tell me some parables as we engaged in a philosophical conversation about what knowledge is, what is true, and the relationship between knowledge and emancipation. The text is beautifully written. It is generous and reverential toward the reader. It should remind us of Aurelius's letters to some of his correspondents, but also of Cornel West's recent narrated intellectual biography, *Brother West: Living and Loving Out Loud, a Memoir*, or of Fernando Savater's *Amador*. This book is more than a translation. It is also Otto's letter of gratitude to all the students, friends, and colleagues with whom he traveled over the past decades, drafting, fashioning, imagining, visualizing maps of joy, maps of solidarity, maps of justice. It was meant to be his "philosophical-theological" testament.

In the following, I would like to foreground some key themes in order to offer some ways to read the text. I would like to begin with the theme—or, rather, metaphor—of the map. Maps are fascinating devices, and like all *dispositifs* (apparatuses or devices), they are power tools and traces of power that mask their own plenipotence. There are all kinds of maps, and many ways to draw them (think of a subway map, a topographical map, maps in Google, or the ironic maps of *The New Yorker* magazine), but what is most important is that a map is confessedly and avowedly a representing device that announces that it is a representation. Here one of Jorge Luis Borges's beautiful stories gets the point in the most poignant way: there was once a king who wanted to have the most faithful map of his empire, so he ordered his cartographers to map as precisely as possible all his domains. So, the imperial cartographers set out to map everything, inch for inch, mile for mile, until the map covered the territory. With time, all that remained were the tattered pieces of the torn map, and the territory itself had become a new land. This Borgesian allegory, tellingly, appears under the title "Of Exactitude in Science" in his book *A Universal History of Infamy*.[2] Maps have also been associated with the tyranny of despots, who map their empires so as to secure their power and demonize its enemies, and with the fiction of the precision of scientific knowledge. A perfect map, an exact map, a versatile map could be taken to be the dream of scientific exactitude and precision. Maps, however, are devices that serve specific purposes for specific travelers. They do not serve well all people, all the time. Maps have built in obsolescence, and in this way they also become archives of the ways we made sense of the world and constructed the world through attempting to represent that world, a point that is exquisitely made by Jerry Brotton in his wonderful book *A History of the World in 12 Maps*.[3]

The moral of Borges's story could be taken to be that maps work only because they are allegories, or twice removed metaphorical representations. And this is what Maduro also means by knowledge. All knowledge is a way to represent relationships in and to the world. Knowledge maps webs of social relations, and in so doing it intervenes in that world. A map does not leave its mapped territory unchanged, just as it places us in specific relations with others, the world, and ourselves. Maps are devices for interpellation. They invite us to place ourselves at specific standpoints and look at the world through a certain perspective, often excluding or denigrating others ways of viewing the world, even excluding other perspectives. Maps therefore also conceal and distort. They invite epistemic insouciance and epistemic hubris.

Knowledge is a way to map the world. This means that knowledge is an active process. Knowledge is a praxis as much as it is a way to enter into certain relations with the world, others, and ourselves. We aim to know, to acquire knowledge because we want to comprehend the world, we want to understand our relations with others, and we want to acquire the resources to be able to fulfill our goals. Knowledge, then, is at the service of life. But life, argues Maduro, is not possible in solitude. Life is always communal life, collective life. There is thus a standard by which we can assess the "truth" of knowledge, and this is not whether knowledge corresponds to an allegedly existing independent reality. There is no reality that is not always already subjectively interpreted. All reality is the product of collective work. For this reason, then, "true" knowledge is that which serves collective life by how it encourages all social agents to see themselves as active participants in that shared reality. Conversely, "false" or "useless" knowledge is that which excludes social agents from sharing in shared reality and that discounts, disapproves, deauthorizes, and delegitimizes the perspectives of others, especially those who are marginalized and disempowered. Knowledge at the service of collective life is knowledge that is inclusive and that grants epistemic authority to those who suffer worst the specific effects of certain ways of seeing and representing the world.

Knowledge thus is also linked to questions of justice and solidarity. The question of the truth of knowledge is also a question of the justice of practices of knowledge making. We ought to talk about an epistemology of justice as well as of epistemic (in)justice, to echo the term coined by Miranda Fricker.[4] Maduro is particularly concerned with how certain epistemic practices lead to the occlusion and mystification of injustice. Certain knowledges actually conceal injustice. Others contribute to their revelation and denunciation. But if all knowledge invites us to a certain hubris and self-satisfaction, how are we to be dislodged from our epistemic pedestals, our towers of epistemic privilege? Just knowledge, epistemic justice, requires that we be particularly obsequious toward those whose voices and ways of knowing are generally silenced, neglected, and overlooked.

The production of knowledge, which is just another name for the process of constructing and/or representing reality in a certain way for specific ends, is therefore also linked to the production of ignorance, or what has been called agnotology by Robert N. Proctor and Londa Schiebinger.[5] Agnotology is yet another name for the "epistemology of ignorance," to use that also very felicitous expression by Shannon Sullivan and Nancy Tuana.[6] The production of knowledge therefore has to be supremely alert to how it participates, enables, and authorizes process of epistemic dispossession and epistemic colonialism. If we think along with Maduro of knowledge as ways to map reality in such a way that its shared and communal character is either revealed or concealed, then we have also to think of knowledge as either ways to dispossess some of their ways of making sense of our shared world or as ways to share in the practice of making worlds. Knowledge is a praxis of sharing worlds or coming to worlds that are shared as we are invited to assume co-responsibility for those worlds. It is for this reason that for Maduro, one of the highest criteria of the truth of knowledge is how this produced knowledge contributes to the most expansive shared good life. True knowledge is about expanding our epistemic communities and nurturing epistemic solidarity, that is, seeing the world from the perspective of those who see and live the injustices of our social practices from a first-person perspective.

Knowledge is a praxis of making worlds, of constructing and reconstructing reality, through our capacity to name that world. Making reality is thus also a making of languages, or what we could call languaging. Yet we do not make worlds either *ad novo* or *ex nihilo*. We come to the world that is already there. Thus, all knowledge is a remaking of worlds that are already extent. To be human is to come to a world that is already there but that we must take up and reconstitute as our own. This process of coming to the world and remaking the world takes place in and through language. To come to the world, to possess and be possessed by a world, is really a way to come to a language, to take up and reconstitute that language, to be possessed by a language. That knowledge is a technology of making maps says also that knowledge is always mediated by a language, whether it be a literal, figurative, scientific, or pedestrian language. As Maduro makes clear, there is no access to our collective, shared, co-constituted reality without a language, and language is the primary tool for the production of knowledge. Epistemic solidarity and justice therefore demand that we be attentive to the ways in which we silence or denigrate the languages of different epistemic agents within our communities.

Language is the primordial experience of sharedness, of being-with, of being relational, of in fact being a web of relations. There is no language that only one person can speak. By definition, there is only language in relation. For this reason, solitude and aloneness are derivative modes of coexistence precisely because silence and quietness are derivative modes of communication. If all knowledge is mediated by a language, it is always a shared way of making sense of the world, of making worlds by making language. Maduro notes that modern and Western epistemology have decoupled knowledge from language, encouraging modern epistemic subjects that they can know the world alone, without refractions and distortion. Knowledge becomes, in this picture of knowledge, a projection in the camera obscura of the solitary mind of an putatively independent, already-constituted reality. Knowing is mirroring. Knowledge is an event that takes place between a frozen and discrete reality and a passive and speechless mind. This way of allegorizing knowledge, however, become untenable when we acknowledge that all knowing is also a languaging, a way to speak about the world, by naming it, by using metaphors to talk about its constituted and fabricated character. Epistemic hubris is predicated precisely on silencing the dependence of knowledge on our scientific and pedestrian languages. Epistemic justice is therefore linked to the imperative that we attend to the politics of language. Epistemic justice is therefore linked to a poiesis of justice, that is, to the practice of making, remaking, creatively and courageously, the way we name our shared world.

Two key phrases bookend this book: maps and fiesta. By now fiesta has been incorporated into everyday English parlance, and even the most obdurate nativist and English-only proponents know what the term means. A fiesta is a party, but it is also a celebration, a feast, a carnival, a holiday. The Latin roots *festum* and *festa* also have a series of religious connotations. The sacrament of the Eucharist, or communion, is both a sacrifice and the celebration of a feast. Maduro, however, has very specific ideas about the term *fiesta*, as it becomes clear by what he invites us to imagine and construct. I suggest that fiesta means, in Maduro's work, something like "joyful plenitude with dignity," or "dignified and respectful pleasure." Fiesta is neither affluence, engorgement, profligacy, extravagance, recklessness, nor is it simply the opposite of destitution, penury, privation, powerlessness, starvation. Fiesta is a communal enjoyment of communal wealth that is equally shared and does not entail either waste or privation; either undignified or demeaning treatment of other members of the community, or other communities. So, we could say that fiesta is the kind of *eudaimonia* that is tied to dignity, or integral and dignified enjoyment. Here, we are to be reminded of Ernst Bloch's beautiful book *Natural Law and Human Dignity* for relevant and complementary discussions of both notions: dignity married to happiness.[7] In the end, I think this is what Maduro means by fiesta: the communicative, dialogic, communal synthesis of happiness with dignity—the dignified and dignifying enjoyment of communal living. Fiesta is a way to share the world inclusively that elevates all and invites us to assume collective responsibility for the goodness of our world.

To close, I would say that Maduro was preeminently preoccupied with how suffering, subaltern, marginalized, and disempowered subjects produce knowledge, with how they also have a capacity for producing maps that guide us to the fiesta of joyful, dignified, collective happiness. Out of their destitution they produce just knowledge but also celebratory and inclusive feasting. Otto Maduro believed intensely that knowledge is a form of power, a power of hope and resilience. Knowledge is not a commodity bought by the wealthy, the privileged, and the educated. For this type of fictitiously sovereign and unencumbered individual, knowledge is what we have when we stand back from the world and dispassionately objectify it and ourselves in the process of observing it. From this perspective, knowledge becomes a form of dispossession and fasting. Knowledge is the denudation of the subject. But there is another way to think about knowledge: knowledge as collective nourishing feasting.

For Otto Maduro the disempowered, marginalized, excluded, exploited, and dehumanized also produced knowledge. This knowledge, however, traces a map out of an unjust society, a society of dispossession, toward one in which we come to a fiesta—to the carnival of peace and justice. I would argue that Otto Maduro has shown us eloquently in his writing and praxis that knowledge in the service of justice is knowledge that leads to the joyful sharing of communal plenitude with dignity. For him knowledge has this communal dimension precisely because it is communally produced. To celebrate our communal wealth is to celebrate the knowledge we produce in order to augment our shared availability of life. What Otto Maduro offered us in this book, as well as in the two essays collected as appendixes here, is a profound meditation on the relationship between knowledge and justice that urges us know our world by the measure of its collective justice. Knowledge is a form of power and power generates knowledge, but at the crossroads of this dialectic stands collective justice. The project of collective justice calls for an epistemology of liberation that brings together epistemic justice with epistemic solidarity in order to celebrate our shared, peaceful, dignified coexistence.

—*Eduardo Mendieta*

MAPS FOR A FIESTA

✿ Introduction

Nearly everyone, and probably all human communities, has had at least a few beautiful, unforgettable experiences of some form of satisfaction, victory, kindness, affection, happiness, peace, and/or hope. A love returned, a successful strike, the feat of getting a home to call one's own, the end of a period of trials and tribulations, a birth in the family, a long-fought bill raising the minimum wage, the release of a loved one from prison, a reconciliation with someone we had fought with, a relative's successful struggle against alcoholism or a drug addiction.

All these are pleasant and valuable experiences that affirm the meaning of human life. Such experiences—and their cyclic remembrance in anniversaries—elicit festive celebrations, bringing together neighbors, relatives, colleagues, and friends in hopeful and enjoyable commemorations. Isn't it true? And, vice versa, parties, dances, religious services, pilgrimages, fairs, and street festivals also frequently inspire and spread joy and hope, leading to new friendships and stimulating the creation of new ties while reinforcing the old ones.

FIESTA, SORROW, AND KNOWLEDGE

In a certain way, human life revolves around fiestas and moves in pursuit of celebration. From daybreak to sunset, we make an effort to achieve that which gives our lives meaning and nourishment, and that which deserves, therefore, to be joyously celebrated with our loved ones. We strive for work, love, food, home, health, autonomy, education, peace, and for the time to rest, play, and freely enjoy our friendships. We constantly struggle to have the reasons, time, space, and other resources to be able to enjoy life without fear or guilt and to celebrate life's goodness without hurting others.

Unfortunately, life often becomes hard, painful, and difficult: jobs are hard to get and keep, a loving relationship breaks up, food becomes scarce, one's income is not enough for a decent living any longer, a serious illness puts us at death's door, the strongest use and abuse the weakest, violence threatens our daily lives, and precious little time is left to rest, play, or enjoy our friendships.

Suffering, urgency, and fear at times invade our existence, thus making fiestas less easy but also more crucial than before. That is part of what happens in this beginning of a new millennium in the Americas, and beyond, for an ever greater number of people: life, and thus its celebration, becomes increasingly difficult but, for the same reason, more urgent and necessary.

Difficult, challenging, and painful times—when motives to party turn out to be scant—seem to be the times when we as human beings feel more clearly, more acutely and strongly, the urge to *know* our surrounding world: to try to understand what is going on in order to see whether it is possible to do something to restore peace and tranquillity—and to give us a good excuse to party, too!

Rubem Alves, that creative and compassionate Brazilian writer, says this in his book, *Stories from Somebody Who Loves Teaching*: "Truly, it seems that thought arises with pain. . . . When everything is going well, we don't think much about things; we enjoy them. . . . It is not necessary to know that which does not disturb our lives."[1]

But, certainly, this painful urgency is not the only reason the desire to know, understand, elucidate, and explain reality arises in a community or in an individual. Sometimes we want to know for pure and simple curiosity: because something amazes us, astounds us, and we then want to know "why" or "how" such a thing is as it is.

On other occasions, feelings of love, attraction, tenderness, or affection for other people push us to try to understand them, their relations, ideas, origins, worries, and so on. Or there might be things whose knowledge elicits so much interest and pleasure in us that we end up surrendering ourselves to explore them with resolve, even when we expect no other reward than to better comprehend the reality that captivated and intrigued us in the first place. At times, the desire to exercise our creative imagination—or the sheer pleasure of playing intellectual games with ourselves or with other people—leads us to come up with interesting explanations of reality, to "know" in ways other than those to which we were accustomed.

In these reflections, I will frequently compare the human effort to grasp reality with the other age-old human task that is mapmaking. For if life is, among other things, a constant search for reasons to rejoice and celebrate, and if the painful obstacles we encounter in life are among the chief stimulations of our quest to ponder, know, understand, and transform our surrounding world, we can then imagine human knowledge as an attempt at making "maps for the party": a sort of guide for finding and opening pathways that will point us toward the good life, a life worthy of being frequently feasted with joy, pleasure, and gusto. Moreover, the very act of concocting, constructing, comparing, and correcting maps can be a pleasant and festive process in and of itself—even though, as is often the case with most real human lives, such pleasure is frequently intertwined with and vulnerable to difficulties, frustrations, stagnation, conflicts, detours, limitations, and relapses.

A CURSORY AUTOBIOGRAPHY TO BEGIN

These ideas are the fruit of a long and complicated history. I would like to share part of my own story with whoever reads these lines. And I want to do it because, among other reasons, it seems to me that one of the *problems* that plagues our current visions of what knowledge is, and a problem that I want to tackle head on in this work, is precisely the disingenuous and dangerous misconception that worthwhile ideas, "truth," "knowledge," and books all flow solely or mainly from the brilliant minds of a few isolated, exceptional individuals. At least in the case of this book, things are very different: these pages emerged because many people contributed to them and pressed for me to sit down to enjoy the pleasure of writing them.

Since reading the story of Robin Hood as a child, I have remained incapable of staying quiet in the face of the innocent suffering of so many people subjected to poverty. That "incapacity" was reinforced early on by my parents and by my second-grade teacher, and it deepened throughout my years as a social worker in the slums, prisons, and public hospitals of my city, Caracas, Venezuela. Poverty and deprivation became for me so much more tragic and unacceptable because they were occurring in the face of the squandering, insensitivity, and senseless destruction of those who wielded the most power, whether it was economic, cultural, political, and/or military.

Such "incapacity"—or, if you'd prefer, that sensitivity to the suffering of the weakest among us—found important expression and nourishment in the Bible, in the testimony of Jesus and the prophets, and in much of Christianity, especially in the most socially concerned Protestant and Catholic tendencies. As a result, while studying philosophy in college, I became interested in Marxism, left the Christian Democratic Party—of which I had been a member since I was fifteen—with a small, short-lived offshoot that we called the Christian Left, graduated, began teaching, and two years later got a scholarship to study philosophy (and later sociology) of religion at the Catholic University of Leuven in Belgium.

LIBERATION THEOLOGIES

During my years in Belgium, from 1971 to 1977, I became, like so many others, "half atheist." The critical reflection that drew me to philosophy (which made me aware of my deeply held beliefs being barely one opinion among thousands) was one of the factors in this shift. Another was the frustration of the hopes awakened by John XXIII, Paul VI, Vatican II, and the Conference of Latin American Bishops in Medellín: after ten years of beautiful public declarations, it seemed to me that the life of my church continued to be one of submission to the powerful of this world and of indifference toward the suffering of the poor. But the death of the two daughters from my first marriage—the oldest, Jenny, just before going abroad for graduate studies in 1971, and the youngest, Vanessa, in the third year I was living in Belgium—was perhaps the strongest push that distanced me from church and religion for five years straight. In 1976, shortly after Vanessa's passing away, a Peruvian friend, Imelda Vega, invited me to Brussels to listen to a talk by the Peruvian priest Gustavo Gutiérrez. At the end of his lecture, Gustavo invited to Mass anyone present at the talk who wanted to come. Throughout his presentation, and from the responses of the mostly Latin American audience, I sensed that the church I had dreamed about was somehow coming to life and growing within the very church I had abandoned five years earlier—and in Gustavo's invitation to Mass, I felt a sort of personal call to go back home. And I did return home: to Latin America, to my church, and to the struggles to make Latin America and the church welcoming and life-giving homes for *everyone* born in their midst.

Thus I connected with that movement called liberation theology, which I had known about and somewhat identified with since 1969, but whose liberating possibilities I doubted until that encounter with Gustavo Gutiérrez.

These lines are part of that journey, and, above all, part of the more recent years of my journey—as friend, colleague, teacher, and/or consultant—with seminarians, educators, pastors, labor union organizers, political activists, social workers, community leaders, university students, missionary organizations, and pastoral agents working in vulnerable communities of both Latin America and the United States.

HOW DID I GET INTERESTED IN THIS KNOWLEDGE THING?

The idea of writing these reflections arose from the array of problems that many of us encounter when we try to understand *how* realities that we regard as oppressive and destructive actually work, and *how* they can be transformed for the better. All too frequently, such realities behave differently—and even in stark incongruity—from the ways our expectations, theories, and investigations had anticipated. For instance, we go to a clinic with a sick relative, follow the instructions of a host of specialists, and it turns out that the patient suffered from a different illness from the one diagnosed at the clinic, and the treatment prescribed made the patient's health even worse.

On countless other occasions, many of our transformative efforts—which we undertake on what we thus far think we know of the our given reality—are hindered, frustrated, co-opted, or they even become counterproductive, reinforcing what we originally set about to transform. For example, we fight for a school in a poor neighborhood with the certainty that the young people who study there will put their new knowledge, contacts, and resources to the service of the entire community, but, a few years later, we might witness the majority of the graduates of the school—with a certain arrogance—turning their backs on the community, hiding their roots, and scorning their families and old neighbors.

From such experiences, questions like the following frequently emerge: Isn't the way we *see* reality mistaken or tainted? Could it be that our theories about reality are deficient? Are they simply wrong? Is there a sure-fire method of knowing what is real? Or, on the contrary, will we be forever doomed to take the wrong road and go astray? Why do so many people have such different opinions about the same reality? How can I know who is right, what is true, and what isn't? All of these questions pose many *problems of knowing*.

Some of these problems have preoccupied me since I began studying philosophy in the 1960s. As a result, I have since paid attention—in a somewhat haphazard fashion—to the different disciplines concerned with these problems: In philosophy, to the so-called theory of knowledge (frequently tagged with strange sounding titles such as "epistemology," "gnoseology," "noetics") and the philosophy of science. In sociology, to the sociology of knowledge, sociology of culture, sociology of science, and the "theory of ideologies." In psychology, biology, and neurology, to studies such as the work of Jean Piaget about biology and knowledge, and about children's ways of knowing, all of which are very relevant to this subject. Last but not least, I have come to pay attention to the history of the sciences and to anthropological studies on ways of knowing in non-Western cultures.

AND WHOEVER COULD BE BOTHERED BY THIS STUFF?

It always seemed to me that these disciplines discussed themes and ideas of the utmost interest and importance to people concerned with changing things, with overcoming destructive situations affecting human individuals and communities.

Nevertheless, I also had the impression, from the onset, that most scholars in these disciplines treat the theme of knowledge in such an abstract, specialized, and hermetic manner that their writings can be incomprehensible to, and fail to awaken the interest of, most people.

What to do, then? A few years ago, I tried to convince some friends working in some of these areas to undertake the task of studying, synthesizing, and "translating" themes and ideas of some of the major contributors to the study of knowledge, putting them in connection with, and at the service of, the traditions, organizations, struggles, modes of communication, and current quests and longings of our common folk. I failed to persuade anyone. Years later, pushed by invitations to write and give talks on the theme, I slowly began to put myself to the task, although always in a lateral, marginal mode. I wrote a pair of articles on the topic,[2] and I continued sporadically and chaotically discussing and reading about it. Then, in 1980, Fr. Armando Nogués, of the Theological Institute of Advanced Studies (ITES) in Mexico City, convinced me that working on this theme was something relevant to Latin American Christians working for social justice. Finally, in 1984, the Ecumenical Center for Popular Education (CESEP), in São Paulo, Brazil, invited me to give an intensive, two-week workshop on social analysis. I proposed to precede the class with two to three days of reflection on problems of knowledge. The participants numbered more than thirty pastoral agents, political activists, labor organizers, as well as peasant and urban leaders. The vast majority were Christians, hailing from nearly fifteen different countries in Latin America.

Their discussions and critical evaluation of the workshop showed me two things. First, that it was worth continuing to work on this theme, but second, it was necessary to deliberate more with people like those who were participating in the course.

A SHORTAGE OF SUITABLE READING MATERIALS

Since 1988, I taught and modified that course many times, reworking my notes and readings with the contributions, critiques, commentaries, evaluations, and suggestions from, above all, the participants in my CESEP course, as well as, later in the early 1990s, from students at Maryknoll School of Theology, in New York.[3] There was a consensus among the evaluations of the courses by participants on at least two points: it was worth working collectively on this topic in a way similar to our existing way, but it was essential to have reading materials (in addition to course outlines) in order to prepare, deepen, and further reflect on the theme.

The obstacle remained unchanged as far as bibliographical resources were concerned eight years after I began teaching that course: the most critical, creative, and innovative texts and authors writing on the subject continued to be inaccessible to most because of a dearth of translations, cultural biases, book prices, and/or technical jargon. Thus, some participants in the CESEP courses urged me on: Why didn't I write up the course, now that I had been teaching it for years and now that I could draw from the invaluable support of various cohorts of Latin American students at CESEP? But how would I find the time and resources, where and when? After talking with the coordinating team of CESEP—and exchanging impressions with the consulting team of the Institute of Religious Studies

(ISER-Assessoria) in Rio de Janeiro—we arrived at a concrete plan: CESEP and ISER would secure funds from a European Roman Catholic Foundation, Broederlijk Delen, and ISER's consulting team would invite me as a fellow in its interdisciplinary work, and would do a critical reading of my chapters as I was writing them. Thus emerged these "maps for the feast": as a collective work made possible by the intellectual, emotional, economic, and other contributions from a great number of beloved friends.[4] I hope that, if they read this, they recognize in these pages both their stamp and my grateful acknowledgment of it.

WHAT, AFTER ALL, DO WE MEAN HERE BY "KNOWLEDGE"?

There are many different methods of cataloging the realities and experiences with which we enter into relationship, countless possibilities of understanding how reality is "at its core" and how it "works," several distinct ways of explaining why things are as they are and happen as they do, and—also—numerous and very diverse forms of trying to influence reality in the hopes of shaping it in accordance with our needs and interests.

For now, and hoping to be understood, let us define "knowledge" as precisely those efforts to order, comprehend, and elucidate how and why reality is as it is and works the ways it does.

If such is the case, we could then say that there are many ways and methods through which people and communities try to know what is real: there are many forms and types of knowledge.

It would be beautiful, perhaps, if we accepted such pluralist possibility with simplicity, humility, and respect. Unfortunately, it does not happen that way in the real life of most contemporary human societies. Certain ways of knowledge—certain rules and models of knowing—happen to be favored by funding, publicity, official recognition, academic teaching, and the like. Other methods, whether novel or traditional, are, in contrast, ignored, scorned, ridiculed, and even, under certain circumstances, repressed, prohibited, and persecuted.

The reasons for such privileges and persecutions are various, and we will deal with some of them later. For now, I would like to point out that—for me—this is precisely one of the most important *problems* of knowing: the fact of the abuse, of discrimination, or even of the elimination of certain ways of knowing, and worse, of the *people* and communities who share those ways.

When a culture, a nation, or a group sees itself as owning the truth, a grave danger emerges for the rest of humanity (even worse if that group happens to have the military wherewithal to impose its version of reality): the risk that, arrogant and armed, those who share that particular view of the world end up inflicting terror, pain, and death on those who view and live their lives differently. The majority of isms in the world (e.g., dogmatism, sectarianism, authoritarianism, imperialism, totalitarianism) are probably just that: arrogant ways of knowing that, if shared by powerful groups, end up being forced upon "others." Historically, we have cases of inquisitions (Catholic and Protestant alike), of the Nazi Holocaust against the Jews, of Stalin's Gulag in the former Soviet Union, and of McCarthyism in the United States, among many, many others.

Unfortunately, therefore, knowledge can also augment pain and injustice, rather than creating bases for celebration.

Another crucial question for me may be the most ancient human concern in relation to knowledge, that which gave birth to all of the disciplines and schools dedicated to the study of knowledge: Why does reality frequently behave so differently from what we understand, foresee, and desire? In other words, Why do we err so often in our grasp of reality? That is, why do the paths that seemed to lead to satisfaction, peace, and joy, so frequently misguide us? Why, instead of accurate "maps for the feast," does our knowledge so often lead us off course, away from the occasions worthy of community celebration?

SOME KEY CLARIFICATIONS

These reflections stem from, among other things, these simple convictions:

- The way we actually live molds how we view reality, and this usually leads us to believe that "things *are*, without a doubt, exactly as we see them," and that other perspectives are simply and obviously *false*.
- Our perception of reality leads us to see—and carry out—certain behaviors as "normal," and to reject different ones as "abnormal."
- We often resist analyzing and modifying the ways we understand reality, as well as the ways we behave in the real world. This resis-

tance frequently becomes one more obstacle to transforming our immediate reality.

- If we want to change our surrounding reality, perhaps it would be useful to exercise and develop our capacity to criticize and modify our modes of grasping the world, as well as our potential to listen and learn from other ways of seeing and living.

• • •

Precisely because of these last convictions, I would like to share with my readers some ideas that hopefully will *not* reinforce the very common but destructive tendency of swallowing—hook, line, and sinker—a set of ideas that appears to be solid, coherent, logical, convincing, and suitable for resolving the burning problems of a community. This propensity may be as strong as its opposite: the predisposition to reject from the start any idea that appears to contradict or threaten our way of understanding and living in the world.

As a result, I would suggest the following:

- I do not consider the ideas presented in this text as "definitive truths" to be believed and embraced. On the contrary, I regard them as provocative, fertile, fascinating, stimulating, interesting, and productive ideas that have occurred to many people, myself included. Therefore, I encourage my readers to neither accept nor reject them at first glance. Rather, I urge you to first of all examine whether there are any ideas here that inspire you to imagine, ponder, clarify, comprehend, create, or resolve something in your personal and/or community life. Then, and only then, discern what is here that might be false, exaggerated, one-sided, and/or contradictory; separate it from what's useful—there will always be something of value, won't there?—and stay, for the time being, with the latter. In the end, these are not pure ideas. Rather, they have been thought out with flesh, desires, loves, hatreds, doubts, fears, dreams, chaos, joys, pain, customs, interests, memories, hopes, and other very human ingredients. They constitute *hypotheses*—still-untried guesses, like perhaps most human ideas—which, for some communities and individuals, in these recent decades of hopelessness and despair in Latin America, turn out to be what I have already described: fertile, fecund, and fruitful ideas for understanding and transforming some of our ways of knowing and trying to change our environs. Of course, for those who fear uncertainty, criticism, and change, for whatever reason, these lines might be tough to swallow.

- Like any other human text, this one is *incomplete*, too. There are numerous considerations that could, and should, be included in these pages, yet, for a million and one reasons, they are not. Therefore, readers can (and should?) feel free and welcome to introduce, at any point, their own thoughts, experiences, and intuitions in order to complete, nuance, correct, and enrich the reflections that are found here.

- The coherence and order of this text, like perhaps those of any other text, are *artificial*. They derive from the knack, cleverness, background, and proclivities of their author—not from "real reality." Readers, therefore, should feel welcome, even encouraged, to dismantle the artificial order of this text, evaluate its logic, introduce and remove what they choose, and, finally, reorganize the ideas presented here in a manner more their own.

- The presentation of the ideas contained here is by no means "the best" way possible. Even for the author—but indeed more so for the readers who come to the text with their own lives, languages, and interests—this book can and should be improved upon in a million aspects, such as order, presentation, examples, and graphics. It could also be written with greater clarity, humor, currency, and documentation. It is, therefore, up to the readers, without shame or restraint, to tear apart this book, dump it, or re-create it in a totally novel, different way.

- Like many ideas, mine are expressed here in *words*, and the very manner in which an author uses words can cause a great deal of confusion. Before making a fuss, let me underscore this: words, the poor things, *do not mean anything*. They cannot *mean* anything, because they are not living, sentient, willful beings: they are mere scribbles and trills invented and used by people to try to convey something else. *We* are the ones—not words—who *mean*, who want to say something. And to do this, we *use*, among other things, words. Occasionally, we succeed in expressing, transmitting, and communicating what we wish to say. At times, we don't. What is important, therefore, is what we *mean*, what we intend—and often fail—to convey. Therefore, I ask my readers not to cling on to my words. What truly matters is the desire behind the words.

- The purpose of this book is *not to present only original ideas*. Many of the opinions expressed here I have encountered throughout life—in the conversations, writings, questions and lectures of other people, just as in the experiences, reflections, talks, and discussions of my own. Perhaps what is most "original" is that I have tried to put together ideas that I have found separately, striving to present them in a more everyday, contemporary "Latina/o" language. Thus, by introducing your original thoughts and those you have made your own, by eliminating and replacing what you wish, you, the reader, will produce a work that is more original precisely because it is more your own.

I hope that these reflections contribute to the creation (or reconstruction) of "maps" that are truly *our own*, maps that really work to orient us, in community, toward less aggressive, violent, and destructive ways of knowing reality than the prevailing ones; toward creating maps that are better suited to produce and sustain solidarity, justice, and tenderness among human individuals and communities. Thus we could find ourselves, in increasing numbers and more frequently, in festive gatherings to celebrate, nourish, and cheer up people whose lives are profoundly worth living. Hopefully!

❧ 1. Does Experience Shape Our Knowledge?

In 1982, when I was in Managua for the third time, I had to get around on my own for the first time. I learned to ride the bus that went from the residence where I was staying, the university where I was working, and a commercial center where I liked to eat delicious Hawaiian pizzas. One day I was invited to a meeting in a place I'd never been. I left for the meeting, prudently, two hours ahead of time. I had the exact address and the money for a taxi—and I was in a city much smaller than my own, Caracas, and where everybody spoke my language. But every time I hailed a taxi or a bus—or whenever I asked someone how to get to my destination—I was inundated with questions or incomprehensible suggestions, such as "You can get off where the Villafontana Phone Company was," or "First go to the *Voice of Nicaragua*, continue a few hundred *varas* toward the lake, and then continue straight ahead in taxi," or even "That's in Altamira East, isn't it?" But how the heck did I know where anything was before the earthquake, if this was my first extended visit to Nicaragua? And what was all this business about "to the lake," "to the mountain," "up" and "down"? I was used to north, south, east, and west! And the damned *varas*? In my country, we measure in blocks and meters. And finally, how did I know what the *Voice of Nicaragua* was or Altamira East, for that matter? To make a long story short, after two hours of going nowhere at a bus station, I returned to the university, desperate, and asked one of my colleagues to take me, by car and right away, to the damned meeting that had already begun.

I spent two more months in Managua. Aside from the sorry bus ride between the house, work, and Hawaiian pizzas, I never managed to move around this warm and welcoming city by myself. In fact, the majority of the foreigners I met during those months confirmed that, unfortunately, I was just one of many "lost souls" in Managua—at times as lost as people from the Caribbean at the North Pole for the first time.

And speaking of the North Pole: in the traditional indigenous communities of the coldest zones of the North—the so-called Eskimos, a descriptive word they reject themselves—you see a tremendously interesting phenomenon that has a lot to do with the theme of this book. Although to people from the hottest cities and rural zones on the planet, everything that we recognize as white appears the same color, so-called Eskimos, the Inuits, are capable of distinguishing an enormous variety of colors, to the point that they have various names for the colors that others simply see as shades of white.

Thanks to this ability, the Inuits have managed to live for centuries in territories where the temperatures are below zero almost all year round. Or, better said, because they have lived centuries in the Polar North, Inuits have developed the capacity to distinguish and recognize many varieties of color where others see only one.

Our life, our personal and collective experience, strongly influences our awareness—what we know and how we know it. Our experience also has an effect—and perhaps this is what is most important—on what we don't know and the way we arrange ourselves in order to remain ignorant of certain things and to deny, or justify, our lack of awareness. This is what I would like to talk about in the first part of the book.

The life of every person and of the whole human community is extraordinarily rich, even if it has been short and limited in terms of material goods. Every one of us has an enormous number of relationships with things, people, groups, institutions, feelings, images, ideas, theories, desires, interests, and fears. All this shapes our experience, what we live, feel, suspect, intuit, hope, remember, fear, and search for—consciously or not. What we experience in the present, starting from what we lived through in the past, that is what frames our experience. And I would like to suggest that it is life, individual and collective experience alike, that molds our way of seeing reality. Our idea of what is and what isn't knowledge, what's true and false, influences what things (and people!) we consider important, serious, essential, beautiful, good, just, normal, appropriate—or the opposite!

What I propose, then, in the first section of these reflections on knowledge is the idea that our experience has a decisive impact on our awareness of reality. And I would propose the following objectives to develop and deepen this idea:

- To become aware of the enormous influence that our experience has on our awareness of reality
- To appreciate and analyze the infinite richness and complexity of the experience of each and every human being and community
- To critically reflect on the impact of our experience on our consciousness—above all, in the least conscious and least agreeable aspects of that impact
- To arouse in ourselves a more pluralistic, respectful, open, humble, and critical vision of that which we recognize, value, and appreciate as knowledge

SOME DIMENSIONS OF THIS QUESTION

I would like to discuss this problem, that is, the influence of experience on knowledge, from a number of perspectives, which, even though they interest me, are nonetheless variable and debatable.

Life's Formative Experiences

All living things strive to stay alive. Each and every living thing tries to conserve its own life and the lives of the closest members of its family or species. Something similar takes place in the human family.

A little girl raised in a slum of Rio de Janeiro learns very early on that the colors of the kites that her friends fly signify important things. For example, red signifies danger: the police are invading the neighborhood. She learns that when red kites are being flown over the neighborhood, it is best to run and hide at home or with a safe neighbor. Or if you are on your way to school and still haven't entered the neighborhood, it is better to wait. In contrast, you might even run the risk of death: red kites might also serve as a warning that a firefight might begin at any moment.

Over the years, we've been learning, directly and indirectly, to distinguish the things, situations, behaviors, and people that safeguard our lives and those that threaten us. This quest for the living—and the complementary fear of our own mortality—constantly pushes us to know our reality.

There are those who maintain—and I believe that the idea is always fertile, when not exaggerated—that knowledge is a skill that at once emerges from the necessity to preserve life and, in order to preserve it, is a form of adapting to the environment for the sake of protecting life.[1]

But life—what protects it as well as what threatens it—is something that varies enormously from one era, person, gender, social class, race, age, region, or community to another. Perhaps this is one reason human beings develop so many different visions of reality.

Food, oxygen, water, clothing, medicine, warmth, and solidarity are some of the things without which every person and human community will perish. Different regions, therefore, utilize diverse resources to eat, construct shelter, produce medicines, and organize themselves in order to exploit natural resources. In the everyday struggle for life, we turn our attention to what seems to us to be essential. We develop our senses (e.g., hearing, touch, sight) and capacities (e.g., using a knife, typing, distinguishing medicinal plants, reading, resolving conflicts), which enable us to know our concrete reality. At the same time, we do not develop other organs and skills that do not have value in our natural or social environment, but that in other circumstances would be extraordinarily useful in knowing our reality and thriving in our actual daily lives.

An Inuit child is perfectly able to survive a snowstorm in Alaska but perhaps not a power outage in Bogotá or a flood in Nicaragua. An engineer exiled from Argentina could triumph in the labor market in Rio de Janeiro, but if he got lost on a mountain in his native land, it is possible that he would not survive. A young and healthy Guatemalan Indian, capable of distinguishing and cultivating thousands of nutritious and medicinal plants at home, might perish if forced to emigrate illegally to the United States for lack of food and medical attention. A Venezuelan worker who is pregnant and does not know her rights could find herself fired from her job and thereby at risk of losing her child because of the anguish and other consequences of unemployment.

As such, real life stimulates the development of certain capacities and organs that can makes us extraordinarily effective at understanding and managing similar or familiar situations. The same experiences, in return, usually impede the maturation of other capacities that can be decisive in other new circumstances.

Life's Joys and Difficulties

Among other things, and perhaps above all, living is a matter of searching for the good life, not merely of surviving. Life that is reduced to a struggle for survival—to stay alive and nothing more—is lived as a burden, a situation of desperation, a bad thing. Such is the case of people and entire populations who suffer from serious illnesses, famine, and physical or psychological violence.

But the life that we are searching for and valuing is an abundant life, a life in which it is possible to enjoy together with others without endangering others' prospects for happiness; life is no mere struggle to stave off death. On the contrary, it is a quest for deep and lasting delight that is shared with others. The good life that warrants being saved, nourished, shared, replicated, and celebrated is the shared joy of tenderness, companionship, work, food, rest, art, play, dancing, and the feast!

At the same time, the good life also requires the ability to creatively appropriate pain as an intrinsic dimension of living. It is also the disposition to take up the affliction others experience with solidarity and tenderness. But the good life is just as much the effort to overcome unjust suffering and avoid unnecessary pain.

I would like to propose the notion that all knowledge is an attempt to reconstruct our experiences mentally, of putting in order life's ups and downs precisely to orient ourselves toward the good life. Said another way, people and communities tend to reorder (that is to say, to *know*) their past experiences, whether individual or collective, in the journey toward what is pleasing and away from the painful. This is why I like the image of the map or plans: knowledge can be understood as the making of mental maps of reality, which are based on past experiences (whether individual or collective), to orient ourselves in the present and that aim toward attaining the good life in the future. But real life is much more complicated. We know all too well that some people and groups derive pleasure from inflicting suffering and destruction on others or even themselves. We know that many ways of looking at life push some people to survive on the pain and death of others.

An ancient Latin prayer says *primum vivere, deinde philosophari* ("Live first; philosophize later"). To paraphrase this prayer, we could say that first we experience life with all its joys and sorrows, and later we concern ourselves with knowing the reality in which we live. Before philosophizing about life, there is life itself, along with death, pleasure, and pain. And perhaps these experiences—together with surprise, fascination, curiosity, suffering, nostalgia, and desire—are what most stimulate our cognitive imagination, our creative capacity to know.

Those realities of life, of the joy of living (remembered, frustrated, yearned, and desired), of death (feared, mourned, awaited, and unexpected), and of pain (one's own, another's, distant or not, physical, emotional, and so on) are among those that incite us to question why things are as they are, and if they could possibly be different, how to transform them. For example, instead of suffering unjustly, how might we enjoy life? Sometimes it seems far simpler to only see what we want to see. We frequently suspect that reality is much more complex, ambiguous, risky, and demanding than we would expect and desire. Therefore, without a doubt, it is more pleasant, comfortable, and easier to imagine and believe that things are as we believe and want them to be, that life is simpler and easier to understand and manage than reality often is.

Something my friend Ana told me illustrates this point very well. Shortly after her friend Andrea delivered a child, Ana went to visit her in the hospital and meet the baby. While playing with him, Ana noticed that he didn't react normally to light or sound. She shared this worry with Andrea and her husband, Ernesto, who both became noticeably uncomfortable. Angrily, they asked Ana to leave and ended their friendship. Unfortunately, one year later, the doctor confirmed Ana's suspicions and Andrea and Ernesto's secret fears.

I experienced a similar occurrence with Eugenio, a union leader who once advised me that the best thing for any union official is to constantly pass the leadership to the members, including young workers who had proved themselves in their labor struggles. Seven years later I found that he was still president of the union. He seemed to no longer adhere to that principle. Instead, he concentrated his energy on convincing his colleagues to reelect him. Perhaps, rather than return to the draining, monotonous, and deafening days on the factory floor, he preferred the life of the union leader, enjoying the same (or better) salary without ever having to go to the shop and with far greater freedom to organize his own life.

In either case, these experiences confirmed what I want to suggest here: that the joys and sorrows that have marked our lives also mark the manner

in which we tend to perceive, see, and know reality. As a result, it is sometimes difficult for us to accept certain realities. In contrast, it's hard for us
to recognize that the good part of our "reality" is our own invention.

Loving Acceptance

Our way of understanding life and relating to ourselves and others—with
desire, pain, hope, and joy; with the past, the present, and the future—is
not completely free and personally chosen by each of us. Nor is it natural,
eternal, and identical for each and every human being. On the contrary!
The way we feel and define what is central in our lives, what most threatens our security and survival, what most attracts and satisfies us, is something affectively conditioned, emotionally branded, and deeply influenced
from infancy by our relations with other human beings.

The most decisive human experiences, whether of happiness or of
suffering, are experienced in relation to others. They have a profound
emotional and affective dimension. Think, for example, of gaining the acceptance of or learning of the death of a loved one, the success of finding
an apartment or the loss of a job.

Suffering, fear, indifference, hope, and happiness are bound up with our
social, collective, and community lives. They are tied to whatever our fellow man, relatives, ancestors, neighbors, colleagues, friends, bosses, traditions, and means of communication define as desirable or undesirable,
worthy of congratulations, rejection, or shame.

In other words, the way we define and experience (or know) what is
vital, pleasant, indifferent, threatening, or unsupportable is partially "inherited," and to a great degree "learned" or "received" from infancy on
from our family and community. And the way we inherit, receive, learn,
imitate, reproduce, and repeat these and many other frameworks of our
perception of reality is through the very peculiar experience of loving approval or censure from people emotionally important to us.

People who have known genuine affection, esteem, and respect throughout their childhood generally have a vision of themselves and the world
around them that is considerably different from that of others who have
suffered overprotection, abandonment, physical abuse, or systematic
scorn. Some women, for example, who have been beaten by their fathers
when they were little, beat their own children and mistrust a husband who
doesn't physically abuse them. Likewise, many men who were sexually

abused as children know how to relate to others only sexually and in a violent way.

This seems to be true for individuals as well as for groups. Social groups who suffer discrimination, marginalization, contempt, and systematic abuse tend to view the world as much more chaotic, threatening, and violent than those accustomed to respect and positive attention.

It is highly probable that each of one us has learned to see, to know, a certain version of reality. At the earliest age, we began to experience that the dearest people in our lives (who are also the ones we frequently need, and at times fear the most) looked at us with approval, took us tenderly in their arms, spoke to us pleasantly, and sometimes even rewarded us with something that gave us enormous pleasure. We were associating a certain pleasure—according to the level of approval—to certain forms of being and behaving. Equally, we began to discover that other forms of conduct and personality traits caused our loved ones to glare at us with displeasure, insult and physically mistreat us, threaten to withdraw their love, or deprive us of things we wanted. In this way, we began to associate different levels of pain, fear, rejection, and insecurity with our attributes and our actions.

Later in life there are the teachers, neighbors, colleagues, bosses, and educational, religious, governmental, political, and cultural authorities who take on the role of our parents and childhood friends. Often, without even noticing it, we look for their approval. We feel pleased by their acceptance, which causes us to reinforce certain habits and abandon or hide others. When we feel repudiated by people who are important to us, this can cause us to change or dissemble how we think, act, and feel. The danger of not graduating, losing a job, becoming homeless, or damaging our reputation can seem life threatening, profoundly associated with pain and the fear of reproducing the emotional rejection we experienced in infancy or adolescence.

Social Norms

Every society needs and develops both explicit and implicit standards to govern its collective existence. They include work habits, religious rites, customs, taboos and prohibitions dealing with food and sexuality, personal goals, behaviors that cause scandals, occasions for celebration, punishments for certain kinds of conduct, rules according to age, sex, family status, and so on.

What is customary and acceptable within those norms, what is carried out on a daily basis in plain view without provoking rebuff from the community, what is implicitly favored and admissible, or what is publicly valued and rewarded—whatever this is, is established as *normal*.

In contrast, that which is viewed negatively, discouraged, criticized, or condemned by the majority of society, that which provokes scandal, persecution, exclusion, or punishment within the community—for whatever reason—that becomes or is consolidated as *abnormal*.

In human societies, the encouragement and rewards granted for normal behavior result in associating what's normal with the pleasure of acceptance. And vice versa: rejection and punishments that result from abnormal conduct lead frequently to a certain fear and pain being identified with abnormality. Consequently, if what is prohibited attracts us so much that we dare violate the norms of the community, we generally do so in secret (and perhaps this is the source of the association between the pleasurable and the prohibited). Therefore, we avoid the affliction of collective rejection. Nonetheless, the same guilt can make it unbearable to continue to break society's rules.

When we reward a goddaughter for passing to a new grade or when we congratulate a niece for dedicating time to help classmates who are struggling with mathematics, we are—whether or not we realize it— teaching them certain norms that are necessary for the life of the community. And without proposing it or anybody knowing it, we are teaching them to know reality, to see the world in a fixed manner: to recognize the need for effort—at times painful effort—to achieve what we want out of life: to perceive the existence of circumstances that make certain things more difficult for some people and more accessible for others; to appreciate solidarity as a way of overcoming particular limitations, and so on.

Unfortunately, in unjust societies, many social norms hide and perpetuate injustice. Therefore, when we accept and teach certain rules and standards, we sometimes unwittingly reinforce what is unjust as normal. For example, when we tell our children that if they don't study, they will end up without a job, begging and dying of hunger, this can easily mislead them to believe that the poor are poor because they don't feel like studying, that poverty is a matter of individual shortcomings and that one need not concern himself with the poverty of others.

I would say that, in general, all of us tend to reconstruct reality, to see and know it, to map it out for the sake of attaining what we have experienced as pleasant and/or acceptable. At the same time, we try to avoid what experience has shown us to be a source of danger, pain, and rejection. Sometimes we perceive reality—often without even realizing it—as if what's normal is the only real, possible, and desirable truth. In contrast, what we have learned to regard as abnormal we tend to understand as unreal, undesirable, impossible, and irrelevant.

A friend of mine, a Cuban exile who is a doctor, had a hard time adapting to life in Puerto Rico. She had no desire to return to Cuba and was making a good living working in a private clinic in San Juan. Nonetheless, she couldn't get used to the notion of charging people for medical treatment or to the fact that some people couldn't get good medical attention simply because they could not afford health insurance. It was even more difficult for her to accept that the cost of certain medicines made them unobtainable for a lot of people whose very life depended on them.

I have an acquaintance, a church historian, who is convinced that it is normal and good that there's a clear distinction between priests and the laity in the church, and that only single men are accepted for the priesthood, despite the fact that he has edited a great number of authentic documents describing the early Christian communities, which didn't distinguish clerics and laypeople, with married women and men consecrating and sharing the bread and the wine in liturgical celebrations. Nonetheless, he is always trying to convince himself and others that these documents are "apocryphal" or that there is no "true significance" in them.

The norms that we have experienced, received, and assimilated in our own world compel us to perceive reality in a certain way and to transmit a particular worldview to other people. Whether this is positive or negative depends—and too much—on the concrete circumstances we are referring to. In any case, to understand our way of seeing the reality—and the way other people perceive life—it's important to analyze what we have experienced and accepted as "normal" and what, on the contrary, is "abnormal."

What Is Known and Accepted

Every person, just as every community, frequently confronts unexpected, novel, and unheard-of situations: an unknown person or unfamiliar behavior, a surprising and strange feeling, an idea you don't know how to react to, a problem you've never faced before, an unforeseen catastrophe, and so on.

If the newness is simply pleasant—if it doesn't provoke any kind of fear—our response can simply be to enjoy it, without a second thought. However, if it awakens some feeling of insecurity or pain, our response can be—after, or instead of, an evasive or aggressive reaction—to examine, consult, and reflect on this new development. We are compelled to try to understand this unexpected phenomenon.

When we try to understand something new, however, our first reference, our inconsistent criteria, our point of implicit comparison is "the old," the "what everybody knows," that which is understandable to us. When we want to "know the unknown," a normal, common, and spontaneous tendency is to put new wine in old wineskins, so to speak, to classify the unexpected into categories we already know, see it as something similar to that which we already know.

My father told me that when the first automobile arrived in the city of Coro, Venezuela, at the beginning of the twentieth century, some people who had never even heard mention of such a machine ran into the vehicles, whose headlights were glaring in the middle of the dark streets, and ran away frightened, shouting, "It's the devil! It's the devil, shooting flames from its eyes. . . . Devil!" Whereas the automobile was totally unfamiliar to them, the devil is, in a certain sense, so well known that in this case he served to understand and explain the characteristics of this mysterious machine.

I would say that the experience of the comprehensible—that is, the process of learning to recognize and name certain things—constantly orients how we confront new realities. This makes it possible—I don't say it's the sole or principal reason—for a government to accuse a new social or religious movement of being "communist" if it emerges from the campesino population and confronts the wealthy landowners. Similarly, that same thing happens with Marxists who cannot understand that what occurred in Eastern Europe can be thought of as "betrayal," "capitalist conspiracy," or a "passing crisis of socialism." In either case, what's new is not recognized as such. Rather, it is simply identified and classified as "more of the same."

I would go so far as to suggest that one of the many reasons it is so hard for us to recognize, identify, and appreciate the multiplication of the *truly* new is precisely because what is new is often frightening to us. Without even realizing it, we sometimes prefer to deny the existence of something new when it appears, to deny that it's new, consider it as something old, and reject it as something bad. And in a certain sense, this is logical: what is really new is unknown. We don't know where we are going to end up; we don't have the words to describe it; and it awakens a fear in us that if we embrace it, it will bring us rejection and pain (or worse). It causes deep and uncontrollable anxiety. Is it "normal," then, to expel what's new while denying that it is really new, defining it, for example, as absurd or—even better—classifying it using familiar molds that incite and excite collective repulsion (e.g., *bad, backward, diabolical, inefficient, unproductive, communist, reactionary, antiscientific*).

Consider the three attempts in Latin America to reform the economy—the Popular Unity government in Chile, the Sandinistas in Nicaragua, and Haiti's Lavalas movement. Didn't they succumb, to some degree, to the same tendency? Despite the fact that each pursued reform in a democratic, legal, gradual, mixed, peaceful, and autonomous manner—despite their aim to create more wealth while eradicating poverty—weren't they rejected by the elites of Latin America and the United States? Neither Latin America as a whole nor the United States seemed capable of seeing anything new in the changes taking place in those three countries. Instead, they saw dictatorship, illegality, totalitarianism, communism, violence, and foreign involvement. And yes, they finished off those experiments, just as they did in the 1930s, 1940s, and 1950s, with the first attempts at representative democracy in Latin America.

In contrast, what's new sometimes looks extraordinarily desirable, attractive, and promising. We are excited by the challenge of the unknown and even fascinated by a certain sensation of fear. Our curiosity and creativity push us to search for what's unimaginable, surprising, absurd, and incomprehensible.

Often, when the known becomes intolerably destructive and when we have wasted the goodness of something new, we stir up our traditions, memory, and inheritance, trying to find something that will help us accept what's new and different as something comprehensible, possible, valid, and legitimate, and that helps us refute what is possible and feared charges of what we take to be absurd, abnormal, or diabolical.

This could be, in large part, one motivation that animates Bible reading in many popular groups in Latin America: suspicion and the necessity that the old book is not so dear and holy that we can find in it keys to unlock our most urgent and important challenges, to understand and effectively fight the crisis that weighs us down in these times, and to assume and explain the new and hopeful experiences of popular community life!

Whatever it is, what I am proposing here is to bear in mind that our knowledge of reality generally occurs by comparison in association and reference to what everybody knows. Therefore, it requires a creative, against-the-current effort to recognize and appreciate what is genuinely new, and above all if what is new offers possibilities to overcome suffering and injustice, whether old or recent.

Certainties

One of the unpleasant and painful experiences we often associate with death is the feeling of uncertainty, insecurity, and confusion. Things appear to be that way, above all, when the uncertainty is shared across the community, when it lasts for a long time, or when it touches various aspects of the life or death of the community. In such cases, chaos, disorder, and blind violence can be an extreme result. Like everything charged with insecurity, it only trusts in its only strength to attain what it wants or it reacts violently in order to destroy everything.

Another possible consequence is that of looking for certainty and security at whatever price and at all costs—and to find them, perhaps, on the first occasion that seems to offer them up. Let us say with frankness that, to live with the certainty that we are right, what we are doing is what we should be doing, and it is profoundly necessary, welcome, and pleasing. Whoever has lost this feeling yearns for it; whoever has it, whether they know it or not, wants to preserve it. Whoever has suffered a serious, painful, and destructive insecurity generally tends to diligently embrace and forcefully defend the opportunity to return to a life of certainty.

There's another reason it's hard to recognize and accept what's truly new when it emerges. That's also why some people and groups cling to their convictions and organizations (we call them "fanatics"), and why they aggressively defend them from any and every critical examination, doubt, reinterpretation, or "contamination" by other ideas or associations. Because, definitively, fear of chaos, disintegration, and death doesn't easily leave people who have lived through these things closely, such as people who have suffered torture, prolonged hunger, homelessness, joblessness,

and the absence of family; people who have suffered abandonment and/
or physical or psychological abuse during infancy; alcoholics or drug ad-
dicts; and the elderly and poor and abandoned invalids, as well as the
terminally ill.

It can also be said that the experience of certainty orients us to know
reality within the canons of what is already known and accepted. The experience of uncertainty, in contrast, threatens the search for security and,
at the same time, forces us to reject the present vision of reality in order
to recuperate the certainty that has been lost. Therefore, we frequently
perceive reality, know it, in the way that most enables us to preserve or
recuperate the assuredness that we are certain.

We can find one example of this mechanism in religious and political conversions. Frequently, people who have endured a prolonged situation of insecurity, chaos, confusion, and disorientation are the ones
most likely to experience "radical" conversions (i.e., sudden and marked
changes of conduct, belief, company, and language). This occurs even
more frequently if the group to which one belongs does not have the
mechanisms to respond adequately to desperate situations. Frequently,
converts—and their new group—will tend to aggressively defend their
newly conquered security, rejecting critics, doubts, and whatever reflection, conversation, friendship, or reading that threatens to relativize the
new truths.

I am convinced that everyone *needs*, before we are able to engage in processes of critical reflection on our way of knowing and living reality, long
periods of living and sharing certainties in a welcoming environment. If
we arrive at an adult age having constructed a foundation of truths for our
lives—or if traumatic experiences annihilate such certainties—it is possible
that we will look for groups that appear to be dogmatic and sectarian in
order that we become grounded. The possibility that upon leaving a situation like this we will accede and/or respect other ways of thinking depends, in large measure, on how "others" relate to us.

The normal human tendency to look for and conserve truths can be
healthy, indifferent, or destructive. It depends. What I want to emphasize
now is that, frequently, our knowledge of reality is more the result of our
previously held certainties—and our interior need for certainty—than a
product of our cautious attention to the same reality.

Power

Everyone, as well as every community, has capacities, skills, habits, and traditions that help them survive, enjoy life, be accepted by the people surrounding them, and confirm the orientation of their existence. Every person and every community has a certain kind and quality of power over the conditions of their existence, a certain way and means of achieving their goals: all human groups and individuals have a particular experience of being able to fulfill and achieve part of their needs and interests.

However, things get complicated when conflicting interests emerge, whether within or outside of a community; when various groups or individuals dispute the same object (e.g., territory, livestock, metals, weapons) without being able or willing to share them; or when an individual or group wants to subjugate another person or community to serve their own interests, forcing the other to produce for the benefit of the predominant group.

In such cases, the phenomenon of unequal relations among human groups appears: some dominate, oppress, and exploit others who, in turn, submit, resign themselves, and give up. In similar circumstances, power is converted into power of some individuals over others: some can achieve their aims because they have attained, through terror or bribery, that which others cannot in order to satisfy their own interests in the first place. Some have greater power to satisfy their own needs because the rest—to save something that they value in their lives, or even life itself—have given into the will of the powerful, ceding power over their own lives. In reality, there's no such thing as a person totally without power, but we do find ourselves in relationships of unequal, disproportionate, and contradictory force: where the power of some is exercised over and against the interests and capacities of the rest.

But whether power is the mere capacity of attaining one's goals or force wielded over (or under) other human beings, what I want to emphasize is that our experience of power marks our knowledge or reality. Therefore, I would suggest that human beings tend to perceive reality—to mentally construct and know it—in a manner that seems to best contribute to maintaining, consolidating, and, if possible, increasing the power that we have already amassed up to this moment in order to satisfy and protect our interests.

Said another way, we know in order to live, to enjoy life, to be accepted, to obtain and to preserve a certain sense of our lives. We do not adopt and defend as knowledge just any reconstruction of reality. No. We tend to recognize and safeguard only those maps of reality that help us preserve the power we have. We protect whatever permits us to live as we live, enjoy what we do, be welcomed by people who really matter to us and convinced that our life makes sense.

As a result, it is truly difficult for many men to recognize, for example, that the biological and psychological differences between men and women neither explains nor justifies keeping women in subordinate and inferior positions. Knowing the equal dignity of women and men contradicts and subverts the experience men have of their own power. Knowing oneself as an equal, not a superior, implies that men expose themselves to transformations and limitations of their lifestyle, suffer rejections from relatives and friends, and sink into disorientation and chaos. Logically, therefore, most men "know" their superiority over women and therefore will be open to all biological, economic, or theological "knowledge" that confirms what they already "know": that women are in some ways inferior to men. The experience women have of their own power can be questioned, or on the contrary (if they submit or don't achieve any victory when they rebel), it can confirm what men already "know."

On another level, governments and political parties—whether right, center, or leftist—present unheard-of opportunities to those in positions of power: money, influence, fame, entertainment, security, and other privileges that are largely inaccessible for the common citizen. The spontaneous, normal, and habitual tendency of those who have access to such power (e.g., party or government leaders) is to take advantage of secure and augment those prerogatives. It would be "normal" for people exercising such power to accept and defend theories that justify their leadership and privileges. Furthermore, it would be expected of them to refute, persecute, and even eliminate those who criticize this manner of exercising power.

There's more: in situations of oppression, knowledge is easily converted into an instrument of power. Whoever had access to certain information may be interested in hiding that information from other people or communities; for example, the owners of a factory trying to lose earnings on benefits for pregnant workers will try to prevent them from finding out about their right to paid maternity leave. Whoever has developed certain skills that others need but have not developed can use their capacities to exploit others, such as experienced labor rights lawyers who exact "professional fees," or a major share of the social benefits, that their clients recuperate. Whoever has risen to the top of highly specialized and prestigious fields in society can use those positions to undervalue, marginalize, and abuse with impunity others who don't have the same command of skill and knowledge. To illustrate this point, in many poor neighborhoods and rural communities, some young people who have achieved a certain level of education despise, discriminate against, and insult their neighbors—or even their family members—who haven't had any formal schooling.

Are there "vaccinations" against the corrupting temptation of power, against that tendency that profoundly affects the way of knowing reality only from the standpoint of power? I would share that perhaps there are only "antibiotics" (and they don't always do the trick). First on the list is humility: recognizing that each and every one of us is and will always be tempted to take advantage of whatever power we have for our own benefit (even when it implies hurting others and abandoning previously held convictions); recognizing, furthermore, that the same temptation drives us to see and know reality in a way that justifies and consolidates our perks and privileges. This first antibiotic would be more of the ethical or spiritual kind, if you'd like. But it's not enough. Years ago those who struggle for what we call democracy—and against what we have come to call dictatorship—propose a second antibiotic, from a more legal or political strain: mechanisms that permit any citizen to denounce all abuses of power by any leader. This requires, therefore, laws, customs, and institutions that assist people in coming forward without fear of retaliation by those in power and with a well-founded hope that there will be an investigation and dismissal from office of those who abuse their power.[2]

In closing, we frequently find ourselves blinded by the shine of power, and we tend to copy or imitate the habits, values, ideas, theories, and— above all—the most superficial of everything: the gestures and phrases of those who enjoy a higher status in society. We "lend" our knowledge of groups whose experience of reality is vastly different from our own, and we end up relating to our reality in profoundly inadequate, irrelevant, and not common ways.

The same experience of power—whether exercised or endured, or both—seems to me to be one of the most important factors in molding what we reject, imagine, accept, fear, or embrace as possible knowledge.

Frustrations

A large part of human experience, whether personal or communal, comprises frustrated aims, wasted interests, dashed expectations, and failed projects. The unpleasant surprises, unforeseen pain, desolate ruin, and insoluble tragedy are, unfortunately, a normal part of life. This element of human experience also has a strong impact on our way of knowing and understanding what knowledge is.

"Frustration" indicates something that we longed for and thought was going to happen but, on the contrary, did not occur; or it's something that we rejected and were certain that would not come to pass yet did. Every frustration has an important connection to knowledge: it is an experience in which reality acts differently from our image of how we expect and long for it to act.

Therefore, in some way, all frustration is a challenge and a risk for our knowledge. Clearly, it can bring us to exerting a great effort to better know reality. It can also push us to take into account aspects of reality that we haven't already considered. It can drive us to change our view of the world. Nonetheless, when a certain kind of frustration continually clashes with our set beliefs, this can provoke psychological crises, even radical breakdowns. Let's look at an example.

Perhaps we have all experienced a shake-up in our trust in the medical system—or we know someone who has. Take someone trying to find a solution (or at least an explanation) for physical pain who gets passed from doctor to doctor. Each doctor, after questioning and examining the patient, assures him what is wrong, names and explains the problem—often in a way that complicates manners—and prescribes a cure. Still, the pain gets worse; the medicines cause unpleasant side effects; all the doctors contradict one another; and there's no solution to be found. With his hopes and finances rotted away, the person hears, remembers, or discovers that outside the official medical system there is a witch, a healer, or an herbal doctor who seems to know and be capable of curing this kind of pain. Despite the warnings and dangers, the patient, now desperate, decides to turn to the alternative (and marginalized) medical system to see if he can find a solution there. Whether or not he finds a solution probably varies depending on his way of thinking about his body and health, medicine, and medical authorities.[3] Perhaps he converts to a minor, marginalized religion—that of the healer, for example—especially if he finds a solution there, and then he breaks with family, work, and ethnic ties and habits that are now more closely associated with this period of pain and frustration.

This kind of process is probably more common than it seems. Less common—and more serious—are the grave and repeated collective frustrations, above all when reality contradicts the official interpretations, shared certainties, and standard traditions of the community. In such cases, the possible changes and ruptures in the sphere of knowledge can lead to serious conflicts, crises, and breakdowns in the psychosocial and sociopolitical arenas.

Perhaps something to this tune is what is happening today in many places in the Americas. The growth of misery; the frustration of the dreams and hopes of even the middle classes; the rising insecurity and violence; the actual repudiation of the theories, promises, and predictions of politicians and economists; the overthrow of the few experiences of economic policies that focused on the basis needs of the popular sectors of society; the uninterrupted succession of different economic policies, each one critical of the one before it and promising the same results without ever achieving them; the multiplication of religions offering myriad competing explanations and ways out.

One situation of this kind can easily unleash a kind of collective chaos of knowledge, in which no one is sure about anything, no one believes or trusts in anyone or anything, no authority is legitimate. From there, among the weakest, there is a desperate race to simply grab hold of the first life jacket that appears, and an enormous disposition favoring radical change and violence flourishes. But there are also, among the strongest, the cynical and violent attitudes that nothing is free and that each person for him- or herself at whatever price, including a readiness for administrative corruption, the abandonment of previously held beliefs or convictions, and the violent repression of whoever opposes their initiatives.

In whatever case, the repeated frustration of normal expectations—whether individual or collective—causes one to question and modify the accepted version of reality. Perhaps the frustration and pain, near or far, are—together with curiosity and the creative imagination—a principle incentive and source of human knowledge.

Contradictions and Inconsistencies

All of us human beings develop from the moment of our birth, and throughout our time on the earth, a certain theory of reality. By *theory*, I simply mean a vision or image (or map) of what reality is and how the world functions. It would seem that most of us, most of the time, do not elaborate, express, modify, or deliberately criticize the theories we come up with. Perhaps what we do without realizing it is to make and remake our maps of reality throughout our lives. Only on occasion, when someone important to us asks about certain things, or when we come into contact with another theory, or when our own repeatedly leads us to disaster—do we articulate, reflect, explain, critique, or modify the map of reality that we inherited from the past and now share with our closest friends, family, and associates. Allow me to suggest that every theory of reality is full of contradictions.[4] On the one hand, there are the contradictions between our theory and reality itself: inexplicable facts within our vision of reality; diverse, even opposing, realities; absurd or impossible realities from the perspective of our map. On the other hand, there are the internal contradictions of our theories: notions that have little to do with others, frequently originating from very different visions of reality; principles that exclude others; opposing values; artificially filled-in gaps; assumptions and conclusions without basis, and so on.

Nonetheless, although such contradictions and inconsistencies are not self-evident—or we don't find acceptable ways to resolve them, or we run a social risk in mentioning them—our tendency is to shut up, to deny, disguise, or justify them, according to the circumstances!

You can find evidence of this in the history of Christian churches. Take, for example, the fact that the prohibition of ordained women in certain Christian churches can be seen as inconsistent with the proclamation of equality of the rights of women and men in the same churches. A group of church historians can even use this prohibition as their theological justification to find that ordained women run contrary to the historical acts of the early Christians and their texts. Moreover, as has happened, various communities can begin to experiment with different forms of women participating in priestly roles. Reactions! There have been and there are many reactions, and in many directions: to quiet any discussion; to declare that these matters are irrelevant; to condemn, excommunicate, or even torture and execute those who preach unorthodox ideas and narrate different stories;[5] to develop new theological elaborations, historical interpretations, and refutations based on the Bible to justify women priests (or, on the contrary, to deny this and present the priesthood being the exclusive domain of unmarried men as compatible with human dignity and equality); to begin, as is happening in the Episcopal Church, for example, to ordain women priests and even consecrate them as bishops; to organize protests and strikes protesting the discrimination against women in the churches; and so on.

However, opposing the ordination of women stems from many different motivations—not unlike every human action and idea. For example, it can result from the fear of change or from fear of women in general, especially those who occupy positions of power; from suspicion that if ordination of women is accepted, it will unleash a chain of even more profound changes in the church; from simple obedience to authority; from resentment over losing privileges, a job, reputation, or respect of others if one supports the possibility; from the conviction that if it's been this way until now, then it must be for a good reason and should continue; from truly finding that this is the will of God; or for a mixture of a number of these reasons, or all of them at once!

Usually, therefore, it takes a lot for us to recognize that many of our complex and even contradictory motivations are the roots of our visions and actions. And it costs us, because a certain kind of motivation (e.g., fear, economic convenience, dreams of fame and power, the simple attraction to another person, the need for affection) are frequently seen as immoral, debased, ugly, unserious, and undignified bases of knowledge and action. Is it not true that, most of the time, we have a confused and heterogeneous multitude of factors that compel us to see reality in a certain way? And is it not feasible that the reason we do not reflect on or recognize this multitude of motivations is shame of being looked down on or rejected by the people most important to us?

In either case, I would close this last point by suggesting that perhaps it is riskier to not know than to know the contradictions and inconsistencies that plague all knowledge of reality. To be ignorant of these contradictions and inconsistencies (and, for example, to blindly accept what the doctor or the priest says) can transform us into victims, playthings, things we don't want to analyze or criticize. To be aware of the contradictions and incon-sistencies of all knowledge, however, can help us to analyze, critique, and transform—with other people and communities—the impact of knowl-edge on our lives.

A BRIEF SYNTHESIS OF THE DISCUSSION

Human beings want to live, not die. We want to live a good and pleasant life. In this process, the approval, or the rejection, that our behavior causes in the people closest to us guides us in learning about life in community. In that way, we construct, receive, and teach trusted norms that help us pre-serve and enjoy life. Certain beliefs develop in our spirits, and we develop a way of understanding the world around us—frequently abandoning that which we do not comprehend and repudiating whatever disturbs our be-lief system. In this way—according to whether our power pushes us or our impotence stops us—we experience reality. From this experience, we elaborate maps of reality that enable us to examine and evaluate our sur-roundings and orient ourselves accordingly. At times, we suspect that such maps are vulnerable, limited, and weak, full of paradox and contradictions. Therefore, we habitually evade the issue for fear of greater confusion and doubt about how we perceive reality. We are developing—and passing on to others—an idea of what knowledge is, how to recognize it, and how to reach it. Distinct experiences bring us to a different awareness, not only to different "kinds" of knowledge but also to varied and even opposing ways of understanding and explaining the same realities, as well as diverse and incompatible ways of understanding and expressing what knowledge is.

In a few words, our experiences bring us to see reality differently than people who have lived through other experiences. These differences make communication not only possible but often necessary. And from dialogue, eventually, consensus or something more difficult (but even more neces-sary today) emerges: open respect to different ways of thinking and living, together with a humble awareness of our limitations.

At times, however, the differences become obstacles to communication and understanding. When we grasp reality in a certain way, we frequently believe that others who perceive things differently are wrong, but not us! If we also have greater power than those other people, we can easily fall prey to the temptation of using our power to impose our point of view on others.

Therefore, in many ways, our experience can bring us to observe things in a destructive, counterproductive manner, whether for ourselves or for others. From this follows the need, which is what this chapter has dealt with, to examine critically—that is, seriously, reflectively, personally, and collectively—how our experience has conditioned our way of seeing reality, to what degree and with what consequences.

After all is said and done, no one is simply a prisoner of his or her past experiences. Everyone and every community has a certain degree of freedom to reinterpret, resist, and reorient their life, going in a certain way, beyond their experience. Furthermore, personal and collective experience is not purely objective and external. No—all experience becomes human in the way that it is integrated to subjectivity, to the interior life of a person. And there, in our heart of hearts, we can reflect critically on our past experiences and creatively imagine new ways of seeing and living reality. From this critical reflection, perhaps new, more open, flexible, pluralistic, humble, and rich maps emerge that better direct us toward truly dignified ways of being celebrated with numerous and wonderful feasts.

❧ 2. Calmly Reflecting on Our Knowledge

In the 1940s, a vaudeville company staged a cabaret in a theater in Caracas. A pair of young Christian leaders whom I had met many years earlier felt offended by what seemed to them an immoral and pornographic spectacle. Even though the show was not attracting many people, they organized a public protest outside the theater with the aim of shutting it down. Not only did the theater not cancel the show; in fact, the attention awakened by the protest became free publicity, and the hall could not hold the hundreds of men who turned up early to buy their tickets to see the condemned act.

A few years ago, I visited a group of former students from the United States who were missionaries working in a poor neighborhood in São Paulo, Brazil. I listened to their comments about how cold, small, isolated, and inhuman they found the new apartments that had been built for working families in this area of the city. What a contrast it was to talk with families actually living in the apartments. For them, the new housing marked a great step forward, accomplished after years of personal sacrifice and saving, as well as political and union battles, demonstrations, and protests. Their dreams of leaving the overcrowded, unsanitary shacks where they had been living had come true, and they now enjoyed a healthy, safe, and peaceful life in their own new, solid, and clean apartments. We concurred that to see the situation as "sad and inhuman" was possible only for outsiders who were oblivious to the conditions in which these families had been living. Even worse, for the missionaries from the States to convey their negative attitudes about the housing was to scorn the families' dreams, struggles, and victories. It was like saying, "You don't even know what is good for you, but I do!"

• • •

When we perceive, capture, and know reality, we frequently reproduce it by passively accepting that reality is as "they" say it is, where the unspecified *they* is tradition itself, majority opinion, adults, experts, or privileged elites. Commonly, this way of knowing goes hand in hand with a certain simplification of reality—trimming and reducing our complex world to the point at which it is easiest to recognize, understand, and remember.

On the one hand, such reduction is inevitable when we make maps, street plans, and other guides, and we unwittingly do this when we accept, without question, the maps or guides handed to us by our ancestors, relatives, neighbors, and colleagues. This would be fine if the chosen path always benefited humanity and our maps served to guide us along the way.

When, on the other hand, we systematically fall into conduct that is destructive for us or for others, repeatedly fail to achieve our goals, or find ourselves time and again confronting unforeseen and undesirable results of our own behavior, it is probably time to critique and redraw our maps and to force ourselves to see reality differently. Other means of perceiving reality will be discussed in this second chapter.

I earlier spoke about how personal experience conditions our spontaneous and "normal" way of seeing reality. Now I would like to revisit a theme I barely touched upon at the end of the first chapter: the need to critically reflect on how this spontaneous manner of knowing can sometimes lead to results opposite from what we need and hope for.

We are going to call the methods of knowing from our experience, methods that result "naturally" and without reflection, spontaneous knowledge. But methods of knowing that emerge from deliberate and critical reflection about spontaneous knowledge and its limitations, we are going to call, as many do, critical knowledge.

By this, I do not mean to imply that some people know only through spontaneous, nonreflective, passive, and simplistic means, whereas others evaluate experience in a reflective, critical, creative, and active way. Absolutely not. I believe that we all use both methods of knowing, and we intermingle them all of the time. What varies in a person or a community is the measure and frequency with which we make a deliberate effort to think deeply, critically, and creatively about our knowledge of reality. And it seems to me that this depends more on the collective encouragement and emotional strength of people than on one's age, education level, class, sex, culture, race, political ideology, career, or religion.

SOME DIMENSIONS OF THIS QUESTION

I am going to begin by reflecting on a tendency common to all human beings, which is to accept received knowledge without discussion and to simplify reality according to one's experience. Later, I discuss alternatives to this tendency that encourage a more reflective, critical, and creative awareness of reality.

Why Make Life More Complicated Than It Already Is?

"Bread is bread, and wine is wine," goes the old Spanish refrain. Yes, but what is the relation of the price of bread with the price of wine?

To what degree is all bread equally good for your health? And what about the wine? Can't consumption of wine lead to cirrhosis of the liver and contribute, in some cases, to family problems? Doesn't the cultivation of wheat and other cereals and wine grapes have an impact on the environment? And what are the working conditions for farmworkers and their families? Doesn't importing grains to bake our daily bread put some people at risk of future famines?

To simply proclaim "Bread is bread, and wine is wine," can make perfect sense under certain circumstances but not always. In fact, throughout most of the so-called third world, a good percentage of the population is beginning to realize how important it can be to understand the complexities and novelties of such deceptively simple things as bread and wine.

Clearly, one problem stems from the language itself. The very words *bread* and *wine* (like *homeland*, *ethics*, and *democracy*) have existed for centuries and give the illusion of referring to realities that do not change. And expressions like "a closed mouth catches no flies" give the false impression of containing eternal truths that are valid for everyone, everywhere.

What is certain is that people today seem inclined to simplify reality, to deny its complexities and complications, and to accept what we have been taught to see as "real." And this is natural! After all, why should we complicate our lives unnecessarily? A good part of our actual lives—our practical and concrete work, family, and emotional life—is hard and complicated enough. Why compound the difficulties we already face? That would be like looking for a needle in a haystack!

Imagining, discovering, and discussing the complexities and problems of reality is something we all are capable of doing. However, it is not something that most of us enjoy. In fact, many people would regard doing so as a luxury for which there is neither time nor energy. Others might consider it a sadomasochistic exercise that would bring only more suffering. For most of us, this simply does not make any sense.

Few people are sufficiently motivated to dedicate themselves to examining the difficulties and complications of reality. But who is? Some people have been encouraged since childhood to cultivate this skill without having received any formal instruction. Others have discovered the necessity and usefulness of study, reflection, and discussion to confront and resolve the problems facing their own communities. And finally, there are those who have had the resources to develop precisely these skills professionally and earn a living as intellectuals, scientists, or technicians. Rarely, however, do people in this latter group personally suffer the difficulties that they study.

Furthermore, daily life for most people and communities is so full of crises, rushing around, and emergencies that people quite literally do not have the energy or the time to get involved in tasks that demand exactly that: time and energy.

Good reasons abound for simplifying reality and accepting knowledge gained through experience without much critical discussion. And for most of human history, people the world over have done just that. They do it now and will continue to do it far into the future! Were it otherwise—and if there weren't people dedicated to critical reflection and examination of reality—our species would have disappeared from the face of the earth a long time ago. However, we would not have been able to respond quickly enough in the situations in which life and death depend on instantaneous decisions and immediate action.

Take, for example, a taxi driver fast approaching a pedestrian in the crosswalk at a speed of thirty miles per hour. What if the driver were to stop to analyze every angle of the problem? Forget it! Sizing up the situation, making a decision, and acting on it has to be done in a fraction of a second, or the pedestrian would definitely be killed. Sometimes it is absolutely necessary to simplify reality according to the dictates of the moment. Only later, especially if the action taken results in destruction, can we reflect more on the details of the experience. Everywhere, every day, people go through more or less grave situations without giving them much thought. Stopping to do so could, in fact, threaten our lives or our mental health.

All people, of whatever age, sex, culture, ethnicity, profession, social class, religious faith, or political persuasion, tend to simplify reality according to personal experience. Economists, peddlers, politicians, carpenters, doctors, schoolchildren, ministers, and machinists—we all do this, both on and off the job and according to our religion, family tradition, and moral code. At first glance, at least, simplifying reality and seeing it as others always have seems to simplify life.

The economist who is running for president tends to believe that there is "one sole" cause of the country's problems (e.g., corruption by the preceding government), or that the solution to inflation is "a simple one" (e.g., slashing the value of the currency by 400 percent), or that overcoming the current crisis "will take only three years" (e.g., by privatizing state factories, eliminating price controls, and freezing salaries).

In much the same way, the neighboring washerwoman can be persuaded that people are born either good or bad, and the bad ones can be reformed only in prison or by death. Similarly, the pastor of a congregation can truly believe that sexual relations without marriage are what is ruining society, and a seven-year-old might not have any problems affirming that whoever studies hard and gets good grades will be rich when he or she grows up. The most experienced doctor in the most renowned hospital can convince herself that the voluntary sterilization of women does not have any physical or sociological effects, and the plumber in my building can surely accept the notion that children must be beaten to become good and respectful citizens.

Let's face it. It is more comfortable to think that reality has only one or two causes, not dozens. We prefer to believe that what looks the same is the same; that the licensed professionals and experts we trust have no doubts about what they say and do in their fields of expertise; that we are well aware of the consequences of our behavior; and that it is better not to look for what doesn't exist and not to bite off more than we can chew, that it is far easier to believe that there is only one morality and that what's good and bad are crystal clear. It is easier to believe that there is only one true path in life and that it is clear, direct, and perfectly fulfilling; that one religion is either the only true faith or a false one, period. And so on, in this manner.

Why Reflect Deeply on Our Reality?

In recent years, a shared reality in Latin America, Africa, and Asia has forced us to recognize the interconnectedness of our lives, across continents, and the necessity of going beyond the given explanations of the many problems gripping us. Perhaps this is why we are constructing or trying out new methods, theories, and maps of examining and knowing our reality.

Let's look at inflation and the successive devaluations of currencies that have taken place across Asia, Africa, and the Americas. Prior to these fiscal crises, a salary of so many pesos, or whatever monetary unit, was sufficient for a decent life. People could foresee with some clarity how much they had to save during the year to buy Christmas gifts for the children. They trusted that studying, working, and saving was a guarantor of a certain tranquillity in their adult lives. Most people went about their daily lives without the need for news on the state of the economy, about the value of the dollar and gold in the international market, fluctuating interest rates, or weekly inflation indicators. Bread was bread, wine was wine, and neither had much to do with the other—except that people would have enjoyed, when possible, having both on occasion.

In the past decade of the twentieth century, we no longer see things so simply. In more and more places, even illiterate and homeless children try to increase the value of the dollar or gold. They calculate how much they can raise the price of candy or imported cigarettes that they are going to sell on the streets. They decide whether it is worth holding on to some of their merchandise to sell the next day or whether it would be more advantageous to reinvest in more inventory or in dollars or whatever. Perhaps they hurry to stock up on three months' worth of medicine for a sick family member. They make fun of the president's call for citizens to save and hotly discuss different theories about why the pastor of a nearby church denounced the nation's foreign debt as "God's punishment for the sins of the world." Often, they go to sleep sad, suspecting that the only way that they will ever be able to acquire the bicycle of their dreams will be to steal it or to sell drugs.

In the midst of an actual crisis, the difficulties of daily life might bring us to reject the complications that come with reflecting on the possible causes of and solutions to our problems. Or the difficulties can push us, in our desperation, to embrace a group that supplies us with absolute certainties and a sense of belonging. The very same difficulties might also cause us to conclude that, in reality, everything is related to everything else. How we respond and the course of action we choose depends on a host of variables.

However, if we are encouraged to develop our capacity to think critically about the world, and if we participate in actions and discussions about these matters, we begin to concern ourselves with the many aspects, connections, and implications of contemporary reality. Overnight, it seems, we begin to question what something so "simple" as the price of powdered milk has to do with international trade, the military-industrial complex, diplomatic relations with the Vatican, a coup d'état in Argentina, the suicide of a businessman, the possibilities that my nieces will graduate from high school, the convenience of using birth-control pills, or layoffs at a neighborhood health clinic.

We do not see reality as simple or complex just because we feel like it, or by accident or because we have had X number of years of schooling. That's not how it works. I would suggest that our relationships and how we relate to the difficulties, novelties, and complications of real life are what lead us either to actively participate in examining reality or to conform to a simple version of that reality: before the enormous frustrations of daily life, we may either embrace a vision of reality that radically departs from the traditions and expectations of the people closest to us or lose hope.

When we hold fast to a simple, common vision of reality, crucial questions arise when we painfully and repeatedly fail in our efforts. We ask, "Am I fooling myself?" "Will reality be much more complicated and difficult to understand than what I have believed up until now?" "Wouldn't it be good to pay attention to this and that and that over there?" "Will it be necessary to try to see things in a more imaginative, creative and pluralistic way, one that is truly ours, rather than attaching ourselves to what others have said before?"

When we explore ways of seeing reality in a more critical and reflective manner, we'll see that it's not about finding the "correct recipe" for understanding and explaining reality. I neither have such recipes nor believe that they exist. Therefore, you will not find them in the pages of this book. But what I can offer are some perspectives that can help us penetrate the difficult complexities of reality.

Examining the Place from Which We Know

Frequently, we try to grasp reality without asking ourselves what drives us or how our experiences and emotions mold and condition our image of the world around us. Again, we see that it is so much easier "to know" if we don't bother ourselves with complicated questions.

But can our perception of things be truly independent of our place, path, and point of view? On the contrary, permit me to suggest that what we know, and how we know it, depends to a large degree on the context, the road we've traveled, and the perspective from which we try to understand reality.

Let's imagine a person who has seen very few Roma people (sometimes called Gypsies) in her lifetime. She has never had friendships or frequent contact with Gypsies. Nor has she read, seen, or heard anything about their culture.

Now imagine that this person is a social worker hired by a government agency to investigate the situation in an urban neighborhood where Gypsies make up 30 percent of the population. Her job is to make recommendations on government programs and policies in that neighborhood. How would her findings and recommendations compare to those made by another team of social workers with greater familiarity with and appreciation for Gypsy culture?

Would there be any difference if the person conducting the investigation fell deeply in love with a person from the Gypsy community? And what would happen if the social worker had been assaulted by people who "looked like Gypsies"? Would anything change if her salary was tripled so that she could dedicate herself more fully to the investigation? Or if she realized that her research could become the focus of a doctoral thesis or book, thereby distinguishing herself among her colleagues and in her professional associations? What would happen to the investigation if she was afraid or too lazy to actually visit the neighborhood in question? Or if she was certain that nothing would ever change in the life of these people, or in her own life? And what would happen if the investigator herself was actually a Gypsy who did not want anyone to know her identity, and believed that being a Gypsy was something shameful and primitive? Or if a private company, interested in seeing this community cleared out, offered the researcher a substantial grant, a publishing contract, and a good job?

Our position in relationship to what we want to know profoundly marks what and how we know it. When I say "position," I am referring to the physical, emotional, cultural, social, political, and economic circumstances we find ourselves in, whether consciously or not, when we set out to know something. These circumstances vary from one person to another and from moment to moment in our lives. Of course, such conditions also change according to time and place, social sector, ethnic group, linguistic unit, cultural tradition, religious beliefs, and the particular political moment in which we live.

Our position isn't static or merely individual, nor is it momentary. On the contrary, our circumstance is variable, dynamic, and changeable, and this modifies what we know and how we know it. Furthermore, our position is situated in an actual society with its unique languages, laws, authorities, and conflicts. It is from this community, with the particular instruments of knowledge and communication within our reach, that we know what we know. Last, our position is a specific moment in the life and biography of an individual. It is the result of a personal and collective search with specific achievements, accommodations, frustrations, and desires. Our position is a fragment of a journey, a piece of a crossing, a bit of a definite itinerary not only of the past but also of the hopes, desires, fears, interests, and goals that lure us into the future.

It is only from our very particular position that we can truly know, and our position also limits us to knowing certain things, not all, from a certain reference point. Although it is very easy to claim that this is true only for nonscientific knowledge, I would like to suggest—and there is no lack of scientists who concur with this idea[1]—that every type of knowledge is marked, conditioned, and molded by the concrete position of whoever knows it. You could even say that all knowledge is one form of seeing the world in relation to ourselves and seeing ourselves in the midst of a world in which we form an active part.[2]

In either case, I want to close this point by proposing a few implications about the idea that our position conditions what we know and how we know it.

If we take this idea seriously, it seems to me that it is not enough to look "outside of ourselves" at the moment that we grasp the reality that surrounds us. Critically knowing reality requires constant and deliberate examination of who we are, where we are coming from, what we feel, want, fear or long for, and how our concrete situation reverberates in what we know and how we know it. Accordingly, we could ask ourselves what we consider important or irrelevant to know and how we arrive at the difference. Similarly, it could be useful to ask ourselves who we esteem or reject as authorities in matters of knowledge, and why.

At the same time, it would probably be worthwhile to personally and collectively examine the particular situation of those whom we recognize as scientific authorities. We might ask from where, with whose support, for whose benefit, with what advantages, and in which fields do these authorities "do" science and produce knowledge? What is the social, economic, political, and professional position from which these experts claim to know? Which voices, interests, traditions, specialties, skills, achievements, techniques, and knowledge are, in contrast, discounted by these authorities? In what other aspects are the authorities and the nonauthorities different from each other? Are these differences relevant?

We would probably benefit from demanding explanations for things taken as "givens" that actually can and should be examined much more closely. Perhaps an exercise like this would bring us to appreciate much more what many of us, ourselves included, have to say about what is real, possible, and desirable. Above all, it might also help us enjoy and enrich what is real in community.

Studying the History of What We Want to Know

At times we ask ourselves things like, "What is communism?" and we want simple answers like, "Communism is an economic and political system inspired by the ideas of Marx and Lenin, like that which reigned in the Soviet Union from 1917 to 1991. In a communist state, all property is state owned, there is only one political party, and religion is prohibited." Pretty basic and easy to understand, right? Nonetheless, this response does little to help us understand disagreements among countries, political parties, and people who are all called communists.

Nor is it a very good definition for understanding why so many Christians working in grassroots groups are accused of being communists and persecuted as a result. Finally, communism, as defined here, does not explain the popularity of communist parties and ideas among intellectuals, young people, and workers.

I am going to suggest some possible defects in the definition stated earlier and explain some reasons it leaves many other related questions unanswered.

In the first place, neither the question nor the answer says anything about who is defining the term. Nor does it address the range of thought and theories, political parties, countries, and individuals who call themselves communist. And this is important. After all, someone like Pope John Paul II, who suffered under a communist regime in his native Poland, or the Russian writer Aleksandr Solzhenitsyn, would not have the same opinion as others, like the Maryknoll religious workers from the United States who were assassinated in El Salvador or the Argentine singer Mercedes Sosa, who was persecuted for being a communist. Everyone will emphasize the positive or negative aspects that best mark their own personal relation with their reality.

To deepen our knowledge of anything, we must first take into account the relationship of our information sources, whether they are an individual author, team, or institution, to the reality we wish to know and understand.

Right now, I would like to go beyond this point and suggest that, to enrich our knowledge of whatever reality we are examining, it can be useful to reconstruct the history of that reality as well as the history of the very language—the terminology and words—with which we talk about it. Returning to the example of communism, we can ask, where does the word originate? In what language, country, era, and group was the term coined? What meaning was given to it then? Who opposed it, and what was associated with it? What were the synonyms and antonyms of the term? How has the meaning and the use of the word been changed? When, where, and in the midst of what social, political, economic, ethnic, linguistic, geographic, military, and religious circumstances have the term's use and meaning varied?

All of these questions demand investigation, reflection, time, and effort that makes defining communism much more difficult. But this type of questioning can also help us deepen our knowledge of things we are interested in knowing more definitively.

Let's look at the idea of papal infallibility as another example. People end up enemies and divided into those who think the pope is infallible, those who don't, and those who don't know. But the controversy can be closed without deepening their knowledge about the church, the papacy, and the concept of papal infallibility.

A controversy like this could be much more interesting and enriching if we examined where the title *pope* comes from and by whom, where, when, and with what meaning the term was first coined. Is this a title always and solely applied Roman Catholic bishop? If not, when did they first use it? And where does the term *infallible* come from? When, where, and why did people begin to talk about papal infallibility? When, how, for whom, and under what circumstances is infallibility declared? Who, within and outside of the Catholic Church, has criticized or been opposed to this dogma? What were their arguments? What discussions and opinions has it generated among theologians in recent years? Have there been any new ideas about papal infallibility introduced by Pope John XXIII, Pope Paul VI, or the Second Vatican Council? Has anyone abandoned the Catholic Church on the basis of the dogma of papal infallibility? Why? What opinions do other Christian churches hold about the papacy and infallibility?

Frequently, people divide themselves or come together against the expectations and plans of their leaders. Sometimes our struggles desperately fail, or we simply achieve different results from the ones we were striving for. Sometimes our dreams are frustrated and postponed indefinitely, or they change and produce surprising results. Sometimes we throw ourselves into rescuing, defending, or transforming an immediate crisis without paying any attention to the historical backdrop of that situation. And results may ran the gamut from unemployment, crime, classical music, the separation of clergy and laity, deterioration of the ozone layer, a crisis in your love life, perestroika, and the AIDS epidemic to the tragedy of a son or daughter who is addicted to drugs. To understand the tendencies, possibilities, and difficulties of the determinate realities mentioned earlier, or any other, it can be very useful to examine the historical circumstance from which a given reality arises and of which that reality is only a moment in time.

Contrasting the Familiar to the Different

In the first chapter of this book we spoke about our tendency to avoid confronting what we find strange, incomprehensible, or absurd. It's so much simpler to act as though the unfamiliar didn't exist. But is this always best?

Let's take the example of a couple who discovers that their unmarried daughter is pregnant. In our society, the parents could easily regard this as bad, scandalous, sinful, and unacceptable. Consequently, the parents could throw their daughter out of the house and refuse to help her in any way. Desperate, ashamed, and abandoned to her own misfortune, the girl could decide, as sometimes happens, to commit suicide. And absolutely no one gains from such a tragedy. Wouldn't it be possible to look at things differently?

For example, if this were to happen in my country, Venezuela, we could ask ourselves if the pregnancy of this young woman was really so extraordinary and scandalous. If we took a good look at the statistics, we would see that more than half of all Venezuelans are born to parents who are not officially married. I am not saying that we should just accept unmarried pregnancies because most people do. Not at all. What I am suggesting is that what seems completely abnormal and exceptional to some people might actually be much more common that it appears, and to see something as commonplace can help people deal with uncomfortable issues and crises in a more balanced, healthy, and beneficial way.

Furthermore, if we consider how maternity and family are understood in other societies, both past and present, we can acquire other perspectives. For example, in nearly all human societies and religions, the consent of certain adults is considered sufficient for two people to live together and have children. In many places, their union is celebrated with a feast, although it is not the celebration that validates the union. It is their union that gives meaning to the feast. In Christian communities up until a few centuries ago, a valid matrimony occurred when an unmarried woman and man, who were capable of procreating and living away from their families, decided to live together and have children. Regardless of whether the parents knew about or supported their union, all the papers were signed or their union was consecrated in a church or before a pastor, and the marriage was considered valid.

Today, certain Christian communities in Holland hold on to the tradition of allowing their daughters to marry only when they are already pregnant and thereby able to guarantee continuity, community, and descendants. In other circumstances, the pregnancy of a young woman would have been celebrated as gratuitous proof that she should get married or, in a certain sense, already was!

Once again, my intention here is not to say that just because something is done in other times and places we should do it, too. No! Nor do I want to suggest that everything is relative, and the end justifies the means. What I want to imply is that it can be good to stop and examine reality from different angles, compare and contrast it with other contemporary situations, question our immediate perspective, and creatively imagine other possible ways of seeing things. That effort could help us to more clearly see what we want, and why, and it could better enable us to discern to what degree and through which actions and pathways we can proceed toward our goals. Examining reality from different perspectives might also help us better understand and endure our failures; evaluate and overcome circumstances that often derail our dreams, projects, and plans; and take advantage of the unexpected events that arise in our path.

Usually, we tend to analyze the "facts" without contrasting them to different or similar realities and without asking ourselves "abnormal" questions. In this sense, I would like to propose that we try to "leave" our normal reality more often and that we compare our reality with many others, especially those that differ greatly from our own. I suggest that we pose unusual, creative, and imaginative questions about the reality we know so well, that we try to know everything that challenges the notion that things have always been like this. Perhaps this method of critically knowing serves to discover unheard of methods of conserving, rescuing, transforming, or overcoming that which interests us about our reality.

This does not mean using a disorganized, haphazard approach. On the contrary, knowing reality requires that we take seriously established research methods, master them, and use them to our advantage. But we must also be able to see the limitations, rigidity, and incoherence of research methods and be capable of correcting, improving, and overcoming them—to the point of conceiving new, more suitable methods that offer new solutions to our new problems.

Unfortunately, this isn't easy. It exacts emotional, cultural, economic, political, and social resources that cost a lot to gain and to keep. Perhaps this cost is even more reason to continue reflecting on these matters, knowing that none of them are easy.

Walking a Mile in Somebody Else's Shoes

Often it doesn't take much to find other worthwhile points of view and ways of perceiving and dealing with reality. You'll surely find groups and individuals from the same neighborhood, family, political party, business, or church who see the world in different, even opposing, ways from the way you do, right? Surely there are many people from my city, region, and country who don't consider things the same way I do.

It seems that this is even truest in large, complex, and heterogeneous societies with people of different races, nations, cultures, and religions. This is the case in nearly every country in Europe and the Americas and every major city of the world. It seems that such a multiplicity and clash of perspectives are even greater where there is an imbalance of power, whether it be economic, military, cultural, or political, and where there is oppression and domination among different sectors of the same society. And this is probably true in every "modern" society existing today.

It seems so.

Therefore, it is quite possible that the vast majority of employed and unemployed workers anywhere in the world, and their families, would regard a yearlong salary freeze as catastrophic. At the same time, large companies might rejoice at such government measures and pay homage to their minister of economy. Simultaneously, it is likely that professionals, intellectuals, technicians, merchants, bankers, and small businesses would have many different viewpoints. For people who don't know what effect a wage freeze would have on their lives, such a drastic measure would be unimportant. For others, it might seem painful but necessary (especially if they are hopeful that the economy will improve within the year and if the freeze doesn't affect their own survival and that of their loved ones). For the government's economic advisers, among others, a wage freeze could be a good thing but carry an "inevitable" social cost. Finally, there could also be those who see the freeze as an unacceptable policy by a government that should be violently forced out of office (and this could come as easily from leftist guerrillas as from military leaders who fear stirring up public discontent).

With such a variety of opinions,[3] who's right?

Allow me to underscore that "Who is right?" may be the worst question we could ask ourselves in light of the range of opinions mentioned here.

Where does such a question take us? Usually, it leads us to choose one of the prevailing opinions, reject the rest, and ultimately contribute nothing new to the situation.

Perhaps it would be better to ask: "Why, how and from whom do these different opinions arise? Who cultivates and justifies each point of view, and how do they pull it off? What kinds of actions and results come with each one of these perceptions? What conflicts of interest do you find behind competing visions of reality? What power plays and shows of force characterize the relationship between the conflicting ideas? Do the conflicting ideas mirror the power relationships in society?"

We might learn more—and further develop our capacity for critical reflection—from serious consideration of different kinds of questions than from simply taking sides. I don't want to suggest that we shouldn't take sides. Not at all. I truly believe that in situations like this, not taking sides is actually the most common way of taking sides against those who have the most to lose. What I mean is that it is not enough to not take sides (above all, if it means siding against those who stand to suffer most). It is necessary to go further, to try to understand the logic of people who sees things differently, to try to grasp how things look from vantage points other than our own, and to attempt to understand who, how, and why people are attracted to a way of seeing that may seem wrong or misguided to us.

Perhaps a constant effort to analyze varying perspectives about an issue helps us, at least some of the time, grasp some of our failures and defeats. And perhaps this exercise enables us to fine-tune our own maps of reality and overcome some of the obstacles that prevent us from getting where we want to go.

But not all plurality of perspectives has to be in conflict. Differences aren't always a bad thing. Unanimity isn't always better than variety.[4] Discrepancies do not always have to be resolved as winners and losers. There can be, and frequently are, other ways of considering and handling a variety and divergence of perspectives. But to do so requires putting yourself in another person's shoes, engaging in dialogue, and having a sincere willingness to grapple with different ways of seeing the same reality.

Allow me to conclude this point by stating that when we find ourselves confronting different versions of the same reality, we tend to think that only one is true. But rather than hurriedly deciding which is the "truth," it might be better to examine what lies within and behind every opposing opinion. Perhaps. I am not advocating indefinitely suspending action in order to examine all the positions at play. Aside from being ridiculous and impossible, that would be counterproductive for any group or person in an emergency situation or disadvantage. What I want to emphasize is that it is a basic ethical imperative not to eliminate or exclude those who see things differently. It is essential to carefully reexamine what lies within and behind visions that differ from our own. This might help us not only to construct a more just and humane society, one more lovingly respectful of plurality and difference; it might also enable us to look more deeply into our own motivations and make us capable of correcting, deepening, and constructively transforming our relations and actions with respect to other human beings.

Carefully Reviewing Our Convictions and Positions

When we are seriously concerned about a new situation, we generally rush, whether with others or alone, in the hopes of finding an immediate solution. For example, we can feel the need to throw ourselves into a street protest to pressure for better salaries and end up defeated, imprisoned, and unemployed at the end of the day. In contrast, when we are pleased with the situation in which we find ourselves—or when we are convinced that it is not going to change—it is quite possible that we will oppose anything designed to modify the situation and not allow ourselves to see the processes that can provoke radical changes.

Perhaps something like this happened to the party leaders and communist governments in Eastern Europe. Comfortable, used to power, and ideologically convinced that socialism could never be dismantled (and even less so from the inside by the workers themselves), they never paid serious attention to the growing discontent among the general population.

Eventually, after repeated failures to change the status quo, it is common to abandon the struggle altogether, to resign ourselves to the condition we find ourselves in, and to miss the new opportunities for change that might appear on the horizon.

Something similar also happens to a lot of families of alcoholics who go so far as to defend the alcoholic, deny the need for a radical change not only in the alcoholic but in the family as well, and to affirm the alcoholic's tendency to always blame "others" for his or her own problems and the problems of the family.

It seems, then, that when we are too wedded to a particular reality or overly dedicated to an institution, community, or struggle—when we are overwhelmed by or strongly attracted to someone or something—then it becomes very difficult for us to distinguish, discern, and separate what is actually happening from what we were taught to see and hope for, from what we want to happen and believe "should be," and what we fear and are accustomed to.

Although it is really much more complex, I'll put it simply: when something doesn't interest us very much, we won't bother ourselves to study or analyze it in depth. However, when a particular situation touches us deeply, we tend to see what suits us, and to examine things in an interested manner. Sometimes, though, we rush to "objectively" describe and analyze reality, to judge whatever happens as good, bad, impossible, scandalous, slanderous, and so on. Then we react accordingly.

Years ago, a Catholic institution in Venezuela was ordered to conduct an investigation about contraceptive use among women of childbearing age in the country. The survey revealed that the majority of Venezuelan woman didn't have the least amount of information about the church's official position on birth control. The person heading the investigation was so upset that he informed the researchers that they could not offend the bishops with their findings and that it would be necessary to redo the investigation in another way.

I do not believe that it is possible to totally separate our values, interests, and emotions from an "objective" analysis of reality. Nor do I believe that it is really helpful to do so. But it seems important to recognize that our principles, desires, and feelings allow us to grasp certain aspects of reality that might be invisible to others. At the same time, they also can blind and prevent us from seeing what might cause us discomfort and worry or threaten our lives. They might also lead us to see illusions and ghosts that arise from our desires and our fears as if real.

I would not suggest that we make a neutral and objective analysis that is free of values. I don't believe that it is possible or desirable to do so. Nor would I propose that we put our values and beliefs in parentheses, as if they didn't exist—and doing so is neither feasible or advisable. What I do recommend, first of all, is the usefulness and even the ethical demands of explicitly recognizing, in dialogue with our community, the values, interests, customs, and emotions that frame our lives and our perception of the world, and to what extent we accept and want to put our values into practice. Second, we should analyze when and where our vision either blinds us to certain truths or confuses what's real and what's not, and then causes us to move too quickly from analysis to action. Finally, we should determine which are the real obstacles to realizing our values and which are the resources we can really count on to achieve our plans, projects, and dreams.

No one is an island. Our means of knowing reality and our actions can seriously affect other people. If for no other reason than this, we have a permanent ethical responsibility to examine the assumptions and implications of our knowledge, in dialogue with others, especially people actually or potentially affected by our awareness and our actions.

I believe that it is important to develop our personal and collective capacity to distinguish the processes that actually occur, independent of our perception of reality (and that in some way shape what is probable, possible, and achievable), from our subjective desires, values, intentions, and projects. I say "distinguish," and not "separate," because I am aware that the realities in which humans are involved are those that most interest us. They constitute a complex mix of subjectivity and objectivity. And vice versa: our subjectivity is part of our objective, external reality. It affects reality; it influences and transforms it.

Let's take racism as an example. In principle, we could say that there are people who are racists and others who are not, and that it is a subjective thing, a matter of personal values and individual worldview. Without a doubt, this is partly true: to be racist or not is a question of ideas about reality, personal attitudes toward those we regard as different from us. But this "subjective" dimension of racism is generally connected with realities and objective processes.

There are objective factors in many societies that contribute to producing and reinforcing racist attitudes, relationships, and behaviors (e.g., films that represent indigenous people as inferior; family pressures preventing a relative from marrying a person of color; jokes ridiculing Jews; the lynching of Latinos). Furthermore, people who hold a racist view of a given social group will also exhibit racist behaviors that have extremely "true and objective" consequences, such as denying employment to a young indigenous woman, giving a bad grade to a Jewish student, rejecting the friendly intentions of a black colleague, doing nothing to stop the deportation of Asian refugees, voting for a candidate who promises to close the border to Latin American immigrants, and more.

Any separation of subjectivity and objectivity seems unproductive to me. However, to understand what is happening and to act effectively against the destructive processes that plague our societies, it can be beneficial to distinguish "objective" processes from the "subjective" processes that emerge from our desires, hopes, emotions, and intentions. Perhaps, and hopefully, more clearly and frequently distinguishing these facets of reality helps us better understand the actual and complex interrelation between subjectivity and objectivity.

Perhaps we'll then better comprehend how and why we tend to deceive and sabotage ourselves, and then we'll discover how to improve and better things for everyone.

In a certain sense, I want to suggest that all analysis of "external" reality should be interwoven with personal and community self reflection. We should critically reflect on how we, ourselves, contribute to realities that we ultimately disown and reject. Does not a father who brutally punishes his seven year-old son for disobedience while at the same time protesting against the government-sponsored torture of political prisoners unwittingly create, repeat, and justify torture as a form of imposing the will of the strongest on the weakest members of a society? Does not a political movement that advocates voting only for "our candidate" as the only solution to the ills of the standing government, encourage passivity, paternalism, Messianism, and individualism, which multiply those same social ills? In whichever case, I would like to emphasize that it can be useful to take a closer look at our beliefs and positions with the aim of seeing the degree to which our ways of knowing and seeing the world are, or are not, adequate for the creation of the world we dream of and in which we want to celebrate life.

A BASIC SYNTHESIS OF THE DISCUSSION

Humans prefer simple operations over complicated and difficult ones, especially those operations that are in any way painful. Therefore, we are inclined initially to see reality as we always have and to perceive it as though it were easy to understand. This tendency is even more likely if we feel strongly urged to take action.

Obviously, it is easier to label actions as "bad" or "good," religions as "true" or "false," people as "lazy" or "hardworking," "honest" or "corrupt," "the oppressed" or "the oppressor," and political systems as "capitalist" or "communist," "democracy" or "dictatorship," "modern" or "underdeveloped." It's more comfortable to believe that every problem has only one cause and one solution and to convince ourselves that when people think differently, only one person, or no one, can be right. It's easier to join with others who share your views, completely trust the scientists and the experts, and resign yourself that "anything goes" if there isn't one true, eternal, and absolute reality.

Undoubtedly, this is far easier than constantly using our skills to question what seems obvious and to ask ourselves about what isn't immediately clear. It's much more comfortable than exchanging information and ideas with others or deeply investigating a reality as we struggle to transform it. It's easier than seriously considering different points of view or contrasting our perceptions with realities and theories that force us to question our own assumptions. And finally, it's far easier than remaining open to the possibility of criticizing, enriching, and transforming our way of seeing and living life.

Asking ourselves so many things, and sharing these and other questions with people around us, can easily make us feel insecure and confused.

Questioning also demands precious resources such as time, energy, space, community support, and self-confidence, which can be hard to obtain and preserve.

However, won't simplifying reality leave us lost, frustrated, and without the capacity to understand and overcome our personal and collective problems?

Perhaps. At least this is my hypothesis here; what I have intended to suggest is that there are times when critical reflection helps us out of personal and community difficulties.

In this chapter, I proposed just a few ways of exercising and developing our capacity to critically know, that is, to ask ourselves about the manner in which we have come to relate to the realities we wish to know; to probe the history of these same realities and their apparent differences throughout history; to explore—in the past and in different societies—other possible ways of conceiving of and interacting with similar realities; to closely examine different perspectives and controversies that exist today about such realities; and to reflect self-critically about how our own interests and values can confuse our ability to capture what we really want to know.

Any person who reads this could—and perhaps should—take advantage of this opportunity to develop his or her own capacity for critical reflection, by criticizing this book, chapter and verse! In that spirit, I ask you to think about what is missing, what's excessive, what should be corrected or better explained.[5]

⚘ 3. Oppression, Liberation, and Knowledge

I met Maximina in the 1960s. She was the daughter of campesinos and had started working in Caracas as a maid at a very young age. One day she heard that Manolo, a fellow Venezuelan working in a market not far from my house, was suffering from a skin infection called impetigo. Maximina went to see him and advised him to rub a live toad over his skin. She was familiar with the infection and knew people from her hometown who had been cured with this treatment. Nonetheless, most people who heard about the remedy she suggested laughed behind her back and called her ignorant, illiterate, a witch, a fool, and an Indian.

Manolo did not give her the time of day, either. He went to a private doctor—he didn't have social security and his condition wasn't urgent—and he told me that between the pharmacy and the doctor, he had spent almost a month's salary. The doctor prescribed a drug called Batrocan, and it seemed to be working.

The name of the medicine caught my attention. I was getting my undergraduate degree in those days and remembered that frogs, toads, and some other animals were called batrachians in biology class. I wondered what the relation was between Maximina's toad and the Batrocan Manolo bought in the pharmacy, and so I asked a friend in medical school about it. Pedro did not have any idea but was interested enough to look it up in the library.

A few days later, Pedro and I met up at a party. He told me that he had discovered that Batrocan was made in a laboratory to imitate the milk of certain kinds of toads. Pedro researched the history of the medicine and learned that various Native American and indigenous tribes had used the milk to treat impetigo for centuries despite ridicule and even instances of prohibition by civil authorities, health workers, and nonnative religious groups. Recently, however, some medical institutions and Western pharmaceutical companies have been paying more attention to traditional indigenous and campesino medicine. Their investigations led to the "discovery" of the toad's-milk cure and to subsequent success in producing a substance similar to the milk with comparable curative effects. That's how this synthetic toad's milk got its name, Batrocan.

We shared this information with Maximina and Manolo. In disbelief, Manolo questioned, "What do Indians know about medicine?" With a knowing smile, Maximina chided, "Here people don't believe in anything except their little doctors." If Maximina had been a doctor, Manolo surely would have believed her and followed her instructions to the letter of the law. If, instead of Maximina, a wealthy and respected businessman had recommended toad's milk, Manolo probably would have paid attention. Or if some newspaper, television, radio, or high school teacher had broadcast these findings, it would have been something totally different.

• • •

Knowledge has a lot to do with power, whether it is economic, political, religious, or some other form of power. It also has to do with other more subtle forms of power, such as prestige, duties, titles, and awards. The connection between knowledge and power is not a simple thing. Rather, it is complicated and difficult to capture. Nonetheless, it seems to me that the interplay of power and knowledge is of such importance that we should give it more attention, especially if we feel that our lives could and should be better except for the power we lack to change and improve our lives.

In the first section of this book, we talked about how the experience of power frames our perceptions and understanding of reality. I want to probe this point more fully, exploring a half dozen aspects of the relationships among knowledge of reality, oppressive power, and the struggle for liberation on the part of the oppressed.

We said earlier that power can be understood as the capacity of a person or a community to satisfy its needs, achieve its interests, and realize its goals. But we also indicated a particular type of power that is prevalent throughout the Americas—the strength of a group or individual to impose its will against or over the interests of others and thereby frustrate the needs of the less powerful. These unequal relations of power and strength are usually called oppression, domination, or exploitation.

In this chapter, we will examine some connections among knowledge, the power of the oppressor, and liberation efforts.

We will begin by taking a look at the human need to freeze our maps of reality in simple, fixed ideas. Then we will talk about the demands of explicit theories to improve oppressive situations. We will continue by referring to the tendency to create external enemies, either because we suffer from oppression or because we fear the end of our power over others. We will debate some links between knowledge and the search for power, and finally, we will take note of some possible ways of understanding the very complex connections between power and truth. Unfortunately, there will be much more unsaid about this vast topic than we could possibly say in these few pages.

SOME DIMENSIONS OF THIS QUESTION

Static Visions and Power Dynamics

To understand our own discoveries, interests, ideas, and intuitions, it is necessary to articulate them with a certain precision and confidence. To then express what we believe and communicate it to others in a comprehensible and persuasive way, it is crucial to fix what we know in solid, simple, and clear ideas. (Although, as we saw in the case of Maximina, this is not always enough.)

The need to fix our worldview in solid and accessible ideas can occur in a variety of situations and settings. For now, I am only going to refer to circumstances in which unequal power and oppression are at play.

For example, an individual—or group—that finds himself in a new situation of power over others can begin to perceive reality very differently than his peers do (and differently than the way he saw things before he reached new heights of authority). In these conditions, a person can begin to feel that he now sees reality more clearly and that things don't really function as he previously thought or as others still view them. In an effort to convince himself and others of this new point of view, he will use every resource at his disposal to formulate his take on reality in a manner that is at least as fixed, clear, and convincing as before.

I am reminded of José, a professional friend who occupied various positions of power at a prominent Latin American university where I also taught. While a member of the faculty union, José advocated salary increases for his colleagues and opposed the government's position on freezing wages. His ideas and arguments were eloquent and persuasive, and over time he gained the support of his coworkers and was elected to lead the union. As president, he continued the fight for faculty raises, and he won!

Some people, even those who shared José's criticism of the government, tried to make him see that in a city as small and isolated as ours, with such a large university, salary increases for professors could provoke severe inflation that would negatively affect the rest of the population, the majority of whom were poor workers whose wages wouldn't keep pace with inflation. Furthermore, some argued, inflation would nullify the supposed benefits that would be derived from the salary increases in a very short time. José developed new arguments to defend his position and joked, "Whoever doesn't want their raise should go share it among the poor!"

With his new prestige, José ran for rector of the university, promising even greater wage increases, and he won hands down. A few months later when the union launched a campaign demanding the promised raises, José's response was clear and final: "The university does not have the money. The faculty already earns enough. A salary increase would accelerate inflation and self-destruct in the short term." Here he was, arguing the same points he had rejected from the government and the minority opposition for years.

Let's be clear that the necessity of formulating one's worldview in firm and clear ideas doesn't just surface from a position of power. It also grows when we discover that part of our suffering is the bitter fruit of the actions of more powerful people or groups. In the 1980s, US housewives in the Love Canal neighborhood of Niagara Falls, New York, began to suspect and say loud and clear that the increasing sicknesses among their children were caused by the disposal of poisonous chemical substances in the canal years earlier by companies no longer operating in the area. The women started a campaign of investigation, information, and mobilization that produced simple, strong, and uncompromising statements about what had happened in their community. Their declarations helped advance a struggle that culminated in some victories for the community.

When an oppressed group finds itself hounded and threatened with elimination, just as when a powerful minority sees its dominion in danger, the tendency to express knowledge in fixed and firm ideas becomes more intense. Sectarian, exclusive, and intolerant views can emerge. When we examine religious history, we come upon the case of Anabaptists and Lutherans in the sixteenth century. The community split, some of the faithful incited peasant revolts against large landowners in Bohemia and what is today Germany. Others, urged on by such writings as Luther's *Against the Murderous, Thieving Hordes of Peasants.* carried out the slaughter of the very same peasants who had been encouraged to rebel.

However, if we are too flexible, uncertain, and open in expressing our ideas, it is very difficult to convince even ourselves, or persuade others, to take up initiatives based on those ideas.

For these and other reasons, such as when language itself makes it inevitable that knowledge will be expressed in simplistic and inflexible way, it is very common to feel obligated to express our perception of what is real in a tight and simple, and sometimes rigid and stubborn, way.

This tendency to see reality as a static condition—to believe that we see things as they are, always were, and always will be—can be linked to the relation between oppression and longings for self-determination among various sectors of the community.

Meanwhile, and without a doubt, every powerful, privileged, and wealthy person is interested in and suited to perceive him- or herself and be perceived—constantly and clearly—as deserving, fair, and the right person for the job. But how do we square this with contradictory and changing visions of social, political, economic, moral, and religious realities? It would be practically impossible! For this reason, the powerful elites tend to fight any and every threat to the stability and certainty of their own vision of the world.

We do well to remember the case of Spanish and Portuguese elites who ruled over the indigenous peoples of Africa and the Americas more than five hundred years ago. There can be no doubt that these invaders exercised fierce armed violence to impose their rule. As their leaders well understood, however, sheer force alone was not sufficient. To hold on to their military, economic, and political power over workers and the enslaved, more than physical force and psychological terror were necessary. It was crucial that they convince themselves—and as many Indians, Africans, mulattos, and mestizos as possible—that Iberian rule was just and invincible. Therefore, it was in their interest to have one sole religious vision of reality that held sway over the rulers and their subjects alike.

It was especially crucial that the Christian monarchs of Portugal, Spain, Holland, England, and other colonizing European powers have total control over the churches of the Americas. They went so far as to appoint church authorities; to decide the existence of seminaries and convents; to commission, or expel, missionaries; to permit or prohibit books and readings; and to monitor and control communications between church authorities in the Americas and Europe. If a bishop or priest preached an interpretation of the Gospel that church leaders did not approve of, the clergyman could suffer a punishment ranging from a simple warning and fines to imprisonment, torture, exile, and assassination, as happened more than four hundred years ago in Nicaragua to Monsignor Antonio de Valdivieso. For Christian monarchies, thinking outside of their box was subversive and dangerous. Similarly today, to suggest changes, propose alternatives, signal contradictions, or stir up controversy related to the dominant vision of a society can undermine the security and authority of those who hold power. Doing so can also provoke repression.

But the powerful aren't the only ones chained to static and simplistic interpretations of reality. Perhaps we all are, especially when we feel insecure and threatened. We could conceivably go so far as to fanatically defend our way of seeing things or to wholeheartedly embrace an entirely new vision that, being more rigid, simplistic, and sectarian than its predecessor, restores the sense of certainty that we lost. This happens often in the liberation struggles of oppressed groups. Take the Shining Path in Peru, for example, or new racist and neo-Nazi movements in Europe and the United States. All these groups have support from oppressed groups with little power over their own lives.

In fact, it's a good time to make the following point to wrap up this discussion: many oppressed groups spread and propose new criteria for understanding reality that fly in the face of established views. One pitfall is that such alternative modes of defining reality often tend to become as static and simplistic as the dominant ones they rejected. This happened at the beginning of the nineteenth century with patriots across the Americas, and liberal Europeans who abandoned the conservative Christian churches of the era. Many embraced a staid, radical atheism that regarded religion as the cause of all social ills and, consequently, as something that needed to be eliminated.

But reality changes, and as it does, shifting perspectives and new experiences move and transform the players participating in that given reality. Most certainly, powerful elites change and adapt themselves to changing circumstances. If there are ideas being spread in society that threaten their domain, they usually react with various strategies to assimilate, discredit, or dismiss any solid and definite idea that seems to undermine the authority they enjoy.

One example I like to cite is the Institutional Revolutionary Party, or the PRI (its initials in Spanish), which had been in power in Mexico for decades.[1] This political party had perfected the art of appropriation, reinterpretation, and the use of dogmatic revolutionary, socialist, anticapitalist, and anti-imperialist language to intellectually "disarm" the opposition during the Cold War, at least until the outbreak of the Zapatista insurgency in Chiapas, Mexico, in 1994, and the PRI's loss of the presidency in 2000.

The freezing of our knowledge of reality is quite often a necessity. But this necessity definitely entails risks for any liberation struggle.

Need and Limits of Theories of Oppression

Feeling overwhelmed by life's burdens and the burning desire to change things can motivate us to undertake the task of probing how and why things are as they are. When we are motivated to understand oppression in order to transform it, it is normal to articulate, discuss, search for, and accept any clear explanation of reality.

Rosa dos Santos, a telephone operator born in 1919 in Recife, Brazil, beautifully illustrates this point. After forty years of working for a company in Rio de Janeiro, Rosa voluntarily retired and looked forward to a peaceful old age. At first her pension was a tight squeeze but enough to live a "normal" life, "without asking for handouts from anyone." Within two years and to her unpleasant surprise, her monthly benefit covered fewer and fewer of her expenses. As a result, she started working in 1990 as a street vendor. Although it shamed her, she also asked her married son if she could live with him because she could not pay her rent. It wasn't long before dependence, insecurity, and shame overwhelmed her.

One day while selling costume jewelry in the streets of Rio, she bumped into a demonstration of fellow retirees who were demanding a pension increase of 147 percent to fight inflation. Rosa closed up her little business and joined the protest. Next she attended a meeting of retirees called by an opposition political party. Ever since that day, her life has not been the same. She began reading the newspapers more carefully, attending meetings and demonstrations, and talking about politics and the economy with her peers. Her life acquired "new meaning," she says, and she became much more active and optimistic despite the fact that "her economic situation didn't get any better." In the midst of this process, Rosa became convinced of two things: first, administrative corruption at the highest levels of the government is the reason there isn't any money to raise the pension for senior citizens; second, the only way to correct her situation was to vote for honest representatives in the next elections, or to hope that honorable men in the military would finally carry out a coup against the corrupt democracy running the country.

To overcome oppressive situations like Rosa's, theories of oppression and liberation, or clear ideas and explanations of why things are going badly and how feasible it is to get out of the jam people find themselves in, are essential. But not only that. People who can impart these ideas are also needed. A drawback of these theories, however, is that they often do not inspire the feeling that there is a way out, despite our failures, isolation, and weakness. They lack the psychological sensation that people need to survive difficult times with a sense of certainty about life. They lack what sustains hope and keeps us from giving up and totally succumbing to oppression.

Without hope, very few people could continue the struggle for their own survival and that of their loved ones. Moreover, without that hope, it's only with great difficulty that someone would even bother to apply the effort it takes to achieve desired changes and improvements in one's personal life or the broader life of the community. Alcoholics Anonymous, Pentecostal churches, and radical groups like the Shining Path, each in its own way, illustrate the hopeful role that various liberation theories fulfill.

In contrast, theories of liberation and oppression are also necessary to encourage, nourish, and push practical efforts that aim to actually improve unjust and intolerable conditions. The struggles fought and victories won for Latin American independence, democracy, women's right to vote, and agrarian reform were all possible thanks to the ideas and theories espoused by nationalists, independence fighters, liberals, democrats, socialists, suffragists, and other forward-thinking groups and individuals.

The value of these theories comes from giving voice to the discontent and expectations of large segments of the population in everyday language that stimulates communication and encouragement and leads people to come together and mobilize around shared goals. Through some or many of these theories, people discover common interests and explanations of who bears responsibility for oppression. They determine reasons for and paths to rebel, forge alliances, and fuel hopes for victory.

However, as happened with Marxism in many Western European countries, the ability of a theory to explain oppression and offer of breath of fresh air to liberation struggles can also become a double-edged sword. Let's see how.

To share a theory with other people is to constantly engage in a process of reciprocal confirmation. Refrains of "You're right!" and "How wonderful to find someone who thinks as I do!" and "Now I finally understand what's going on!" are common. This is even more so with marginalized and persecuted minorities who tend to be much more closed, in the sense that they seldom open up to a vision of their lives other than their own, and they tend to develop very strong internal cohesion, with few openings to outsiders.

When it's shared far and wide within an oppressed group, an explicit theory that nourishes the hopes and promise of a better life tends to be accepted not as a theory but as a vibrant and vital reality. In such a situation, a group that shares a theoretical framework constantly confirms, as much in victory as in losses, and rejects almost any attempt to criticize or transform dearly held views. When we hold fast to a certain vision of reality, we resist opening it up, enriching, transforming, or substituting it even when experience and "outside" opinion point to the need to revise our views. Unfortunately, we observe and interpret all reality, including experiences or opinions that run counter to our own, through the same lens until it becomes further confirmation of our way of seeing the world.

On the left, of course, it's much the same. Many Marxist groups involved in armed struggle in Latin America see in every overthrow of a democratic government confirmation that power will not concede peacefully. In democratic victories, they see democracy as only serving the bourgeoisie and regard losses suffered in armed struggle as momentary setbacks on the only road to popular triumph. And in every criticism of their narrow vision, they see betrayal. As we say in my country: *Si no te pela el chingo, te pela el sin nariz,* "if the snub-nosed guy doesn't get you, the one without a nose will."

We can likewise find analogies among neoliberals throughout the Americas who are convinced that only privatization of industry can stimulate economic prosperity and end the misery endured by so many people. Just look at the so-called Asian tigers of Singapore, South Korea, Indonesia, and Taiwan. These countries, with supposedly fewer resources and greater poverty than ours, say they will become "modernized" and end poverty in a matter of a few years, thanks to "privatization." When it's mentioned that these countries "developed" under military dictatorship, with innumerable victims, some people admit that it's true but argue that "it's necessary to first liberalize the economy and then pursue political democracy."[2] If you point out that in Taiwan, the four largest industries—steel, oil, navigation, and metalworks—are state owned, and that the state bureaucracy is huge in several of these countries, they dismiss and distrust the facts. When someone points out that Cuba was able to satisfy the basic needs of its people without privatization, many react by condemning the existence of the military dictatorship there! Now that the Asian tigers are in a crisis similar to Latin America in the 1980s, neoliberals are quiet, and they argue that it's merely a accident, a passing phase. Once again, there's no way or manner to open a theory so closed to reality.

For some religious groups who are successful among the very poor, the "world crisis" and all suffering are the result (both the effect and the punishment) of our individual sins and announce the coming Final Judgment. Only those who join with one of these groups, accepting their dogma and living according to their rules, will be saved. If a person is cured in one of their healing rites, it confirms the holiness of the group and their vision of reality. If, however, a sick person is not cured of a physical ailment, it will be interpreted as a spiritual cure, the presence of the devil, punishment, or the first step toward true divine salvation. If many people join the group, it confirms the rest of their commitment. In the event that some leave the cult, it can be seen as the influence of Satan. It's very difficult to admit the need to see things differently. An extreme case was the religious group from the United States that was led to Guyana by Jim Jones. Hundreds of "believers" chose collective suicide before questioning their own ideas and beliefs.

Clearly, it's not easy to see our theories as nothing more than temporary maps of one slice of reality or to regard them as valuable only as long as reality stays the same. This is especially difficult when there is misery and persecution. But if we resist a critique and transformation of our theories of oppression and liberation, they can cease to be tools to abolish oppressive conditions and instead can become real obstacles to our liberation.

Who Is Responsible for Our Burdens?

Experiencing oppression, insecurity, and injustice, and living in fear of losing loved ones, friendships, property, employment, respect, and possibly life itself, seem time and again to bring us to search for the causes of our problems—with the hope that our quest will be the way to start to free ourselves from what torments us.

The search for the roots of our misery, insecurity, and suffering can carry us along different paths. For people who were abused during childhood, the "easiest" and most self destructive route can lead to blaming oneself as the cause of one's afflictions. This is even more difficult for individuals who hoist on their shoulders responsibility for their afflictions. Another way is to regard pain as well-deserved punishment—from God, nature, luck, or economic laws—because of sins, errors, shortcomings, or purely personal defects, such as a lack of intelligence, cowardice, laziness, inferiority, or not having studied or worked hard enough. Beyond our own responsibility—but also out of our reach and our capacity to change things—it is common to trace the source of our suffering to uncontrollable forces such as destiny, karma, the stars, bad luck, "the times," world crisis, and so on. The historical period, Divine Providence, the laws of the market, or the superiority of those who have the power could also be the culprits.

Another method for locating the source of our problems is to try to identify those factors (outside of ourselves but still within our ability to influence reality) that cause children and others we consider innocent victims to suffer. We can place a lot of the explanations into this category that define, conceive of, or create the "other," a personal or collective enemy that is human and vulnerable, as the main cause of our calamities. Whether it is the bourgeoisie, the communists, the imperialists, the immigrants, or some other group, the reasoning goes, the enemy should be overthrown so that our trials and tribulations will come to an end.

It seems to me that practically all these forms of understanding the roots of oppression and human misery can be, and have been, managed by a powerful minority in order to consolidate their control over others. Only a precious few of these hypotheses have been suitable for promoting successful liberation movements among the oppressed.

One of the ways the oppressed define the causes of their collective misfortunes and longings is by finding and naming an enemy. Patriotic forces from various regions of the Americas in the eighteenth and nineteenth centuries found a foe they needed to defeat in the European empires of England, France, Spain, Holland, and Portugal, and they overthrew them! Wars of independence and democratic struggles against dictators are clear instances of when defining "us" and "them" as *allies* and *enemies* can truly help the oppressed succeed in obtaining their interests.

Nonetheless, a definition of *enemies* and *allies* that is too strict and constrained can easily cause confusion, new injustices, and grave defeats, especially in the long run. Why? In part because those "enemies" are alive. They can change, suffer internal conflicts, split up, and become weakened, as we saw in the dizzying changes wrought by Mikhail Gorbachev and other "communist enemies" in Eastern Europe, and also in the transformation made by George H. W. Bush and his son George W. Bush of old friends like Manuel Noriega and Saddam Hussein into archenemies.

As the refrain goes, "Everything isn't always as it appears to be." That is to say that not every person who falls under our definition of *enemy* is exclusively and totally against our interests and ideas. Nor is every one of "us" always pure and innocent, completely dedicated to the cause, without weaknesses or ambiguities of any kind. (It seems that the powerful know and take advantage of this human reality more effectively than the oppressed.) To threateningly point to enemies on all fronts—and welcome as allies only those who submit 100 percent to our demands—can produce exactly what we don't want: an increase in the number and cohesion of our "enemies" and a reduction of our "allies" to a minimum.

Coincidence and cooperation with "others" can come about only by approaching one another through respectful dialogue, relative concessions, and the willingness to enrich, bend, and downplay our idea of who our actual enemies and our potential allies are (and in what ways, for what purpose, and to what extent are some our enemies and others our allies).

As we can see in this camp and many others, knowledge of reality becomes part of reality itself, and it can change what is known.[3] "Knowing" someone as an ally, including someone who feels like our enemy, will influence how we act toward that person or group. At the same time, it will also condition the perception that group or person has of us. Continuing in the same vein, this dynamic can bring about a transformation of a potential enemy into a true ally.

That's why I like talking about constructing reality, and by that I am referring to the process of knowing what's real. First, because when we are aware of reality, like when we make a map, we are already in some way changing and inventing it through the steps of elimination, selection, setting priorities, and completion. Second, because once a certain clear and fixed image, or specific map, of reality is constructed, "knowledge" of what's real will contribute to what we set out to recover, mend, and re-create through our actions.

As for knowledge at the root of oppression, I want to suggest that constructing an enemy in order to understand oppression and successfully struggle against it may be inevitable. Perhaps. But I am not entirely sure. What I do feel certain of is that no concept of enemy or ally exhausts the reality of social conflicts. Every enemy and every ally is an endlessly more varied, mutable, rich, and complex reality that any concept or theory would ever allow.

Just the same, if what really interests us—much more than creating perfect theories, being right, and winning debates—is to contribute to overcoming oppressive relationships, I would suggest that we constantly and critically revise the concepts and theories we use to examine the causes and ways out of oppressive relationships. In particular, I would propose critically revising every idea that reduces the enemy to a fixed reality that is totally outside of ourselves. I would propose the same for every theory that idealizes "us" and presents our allies in a static and idealized way. It seems to me that such ideas and theories can contribute much more to the consolidation of oppression—and the creation of new injustices—than providing solutions to the difficult situations we find ourselves in at the start of the new millennium.

Isn't Knowledge Only for Intellectuals?

When I wrote the first version of this book, I read in a newspaper that quinine—the base of the few medicines effective in treating malaria—"has been known by Europeans since 1630, when the Indians of South America showed Jesuit missionaries that the substance cured fevers."[4] I feared that this commentary would prompt many people to say, like Manolo said about Maximina, "What do Indians know about medicine?"

One of the problems of human knowledge is that, all too frequently, we discredit our own and others' capacity to actively and creatively participate in intellectual activities, such as the construction, critique, and transformation of knowledge. Habitually, we think that only the scientists, intellectuals, and other experts truly know or at least know what is really important.

Said another way, we commonly renounce our own responsibility to know and turn it over to the "experts." We delegate the power of deciding what is certain, safe, and true, and what should be done, to the specialists. We accept that the engineers, politicians, doctors, theologians, and other professionals be remunerated far above what's common among mere mortals (not only in money but also in prestige, power, stability, and security) for assuming that responsibility. We even participate, wittingly and unwittingly, in campaigns to keep "nonprofessionals" out of the hallowed halls of knowledge. Again, "What do Indians know about medicine?"

Why should this be?

Clearly, it's partly because of laziness. It's easier for others to decide what we should believe and do. If they make a mistake, we have someone to blame. If they are right, we all benefit. Also, it's partly because "that's what everybody thinks," and it seems better to avoid the innumerable risks of swimming against the current ("Where is Vicente going? Where everyone is going!").

But there are other reasons for this handing over of knowledge to professionals that seems typical of societies in which power is concentrated in few hands. A number of years ago, my friend the priest and theologian Pablo Richard told me about an experience that happened one night during Bible study in a popular congregation. After reading a passage from the Gospel, Pablo asked if someone would share their opinions about the text. One by one, everyone entered into an animated conversation about the Bible passage—except for an older man seated far behind everyone else with his head drooping. Wanting to hear his opinion, Pablo asked him to participate. Several people in the group turned around and encouraged him to express his point of view. The old man covered his face and began to sob. Pablo, fearing he had offended or disturbed the man, approached him and asked forgiveness and inquired how he could help. "No, Father," the man said, "what's happening is that this is the first time in my life that anyone has asked my opinion about something important."

To creatively and actively participate in the collective responsibility of building, critiquing, and transforming our knowledge demands resources. It requires time, physical energy, suitable space—such as a quiet house or patio, classroom, temple, or theater—and the habitual practice of self-expression, reading, or writing. It may call for basic materials such as pencils, paper, a camera, computers, or a musical instrument, according to our skills and inclinations. Without a doubt, it requires recognition and affirmation from the community and a healthy dose of self-confidence and self-esteem.

Yet the majority of people in the Americas must deal with difficult obstacles to developing their intellectual potential and their ability to contribute to the construction of knowledge. Most face dire shortages of the aforementioned resources. Against tremendous odds, however, many of our people exercise their intellectual capacity, even if only in limited circles among few relatives and neighbors or quietly to themselves.

Most, if not all, people have needs (e.g., educational, recreational, sociological, work, housing, health, religious, communication) that require intellectual production and the creative work of articulating, critiquing, and transforming knowledge. What happens when people in dire straits lack the basic resources to satisfy their needs on their own?

I think that the majority of our people are constantly forced to turn to those who have the time, energy, space, discipline, resources, recognition, and self-esteem to become the "experts," "intellectuals," or other "professionals" who enjoy self-confidence and respect from their peers and the public.

This would not be a problem if the intellectual elites and professional class always had corresponding, complementary, or at least compatible interests with the majority of nonprofessional workers and their families. But this is rare. We are well aware that the habits of money, power, fame, and other privileges often bring many professionals—engineers, lawyers, pastors, economists, writers, and politicians alike—to perceive, present, and manage reality to serve their own interests, against the aspirations of their clients, the public, readers, patients, and others.[5]

Furthermore, just as the makers of different kinds of cigarettes compete among themselves to convince each and every one of us that their product is "the best," different professions (and different "experts") compete to try to sell us their ideas and services. Tragically, just as cigarette makers could care less about public health, a good number of our "experts" don't care much about what happens to their clients, patients, and consumers. What interests them is the advantage, profit, and other benefits they can derive from our necessities and difficulties.

And I insist that this isn't a matter of personal good or evil. No! It is a question of how the professional system actually functions in our Western urban societies. Professionals who function under a different logic, with the well-being of their clients and community at heart, tend to lose the respect and authorization from their colleagues—and even from the public!

Part of the problem is that, in handing over our intellectual power to the "experts," we are constantly running the risk that this power will be used against our interests and solely for the personal benefit of those "experts."

But another part of the problem, one that might be more relevant for the theme of these reflections, is that the construction, critique, and transformation of our worldviews, of our awareness of reality, are made with neither our control nor our participation. Furthermore, what we generally accept as "knowledge"—and that often governs our beliefs, studies, work, food, health, and so on—have been made by people who don't know or share (and often don't respect) the circumstances of life experienced by the majority of the world's population. To put it simply, the heads that think for us—independently of their intentions—work from perspectives and interests that are rarely ours, the majority's.

In movements and efforts aimed at the transformation of community life, new intellectual needs arise, such as understanding what and why society should and could be changed; determining which traditions we should deepen and develop and which should we leave behind; and creating new symbols, rites, and other cultural expressions that show and improve the prospects for a better life.

Such needs demand intellectual work: investigation, comparison, imagination, creation, organization, and communication. And just as in these movements not everyone develops their abilities and inclinations, there is also a shortage of intellectuals, those experienced individuals and groups who are inclined and dedicated to the task of constructing, critiquing, and transforming what the community knows. People are needed who are able to gather, articulate, and communicate visions of reality that contribute to the realization of the needs and hopes of the oppressed.

For intellectuals to emerge in the midst of these movements, all of the ambiguities mentioned already also arise. Using one's capacity and intellectual production to make up for economic shortages or powerlessness is a permanent temptation: to become the "little doctor" of the community, to demand privileges that are inaccessible to most people, to refuse fraternal criticism, to isolate and place one's self above others, to use the pressure and popular organizations for purely individual gain. These are some of the numerous temptations of any intellectual—composer, writer, singer, doctor, journalist, lawyers, accountant—who tries or claims to put his or her talents at the service of liberation movements of the oppressed.

But there is no need to become alarmed. Every remedy, poorly applied, can hurt whatever it seeks to cure, and this also happens with intellectuals and intellectual work. Perhaps the thing is to administer the medicine carefully, periodically evaluating its effects in dialogue with the community to see if the results really are what is desired, and if not, to determine what to do next.

Practical Context and Theoretical Knowledge

How do we know if knowledge is "true" or not, or what significance this "true" knowledge really has? There, in a nutshell, you have one of the oldest problems of human knowledge (which I won't pretend to resolve or even less offer a "definitive solution"—in these reflections).

Philosophers frequently tend to "resolve" the problem as if truth and falsehood were characteristics of "pure ideas" expressed in worlds where knowledge is separated from the activity that engendered awareness in the first place. To illustrate my point, whether it's true, for example, that humanity constantly progresses will be discussed but rarely probed with questions such as, True in what sense? To what point? Since when? Where did this idea arise? With what consequences? For whom? Even philosophers who worry about referring all "truth" to material reality at times regard experience as one and the same for all people, regardless of gender, age, culture, or physical, social, political, economic, or religious circumstance—and without asking themselves anything about the experience itself that resulted in certain knowledge.

Perhaps before asking ourselves how we know if knowledge is or isn't true and what "true knowledge" actually means, we could pose other kinds of questions and concerns. Why, for example, reduce knowledge to phrases and ideas separated from the concrete human context where this knowledge originates and functions? Perhaps it makes more sense to remember that knowledge is part of a dynamic social process that arises from a concrete human collective.

In that light, knowledge is not so much a matter of abstract truth sealed in a vacuum and separated from the real human dynamic where knowledge originates. Not at all. Here, it is better to try to understand the sense and significance of knowing reality in the community in which it comes about. What real changes does this new knowledge introduce in relation to previously held views about reality? Where does this new perception take us? To what point does this awareness help people reach what they are seeking? What consequences—seen and unforeseen, welcome or unwelcome and destructive for others, irreversible or not—result from this knowledge?

Determining what is "generally" true or false about knowledge is not a schematic, abstract exercise. Instead, we confront a real problem of where, how, and for what purpose our knowledge arises. We are face-to-face with the challenge of responsibly dealing with the practical consequences of our way of perceiving reality. We must take up the challenge of evaluating the extent to which our knowledge helps or hinders us in achieving what we were looking for in the first place.

Of course this other perspective, like any other, can be underestimated, simplified, mocked, and ridiculed. With good reason and quite frequently, human beings give enormous importance to the practical consequences of knowledge as at least one of the criteria for distinguishing "true" and "false." I think it's interesting to think about this for a while.[6]

Life, happiness, hope, fear, pain, and death are a central part of everyday human existence. They have to do with the goals, accomplishments, efforts, deceptions, and failures that mark daily life. Knowledge isn't distant from the concrete, practical worries of real life. On the contrary, I would suggest that the effort to know reality is interwoven with the vital desires of daily life and is at once influencing and being influenced by these longings.

The economist who is promoted in her work for having contributed to increasing industry earnings will feel confident that her reading of the economy is "correct" and that whoever refutes her claim is wrong. The doctor and the parent who see all their efforts fail to diagnose and cure a sick daughter can begin to seriously doubt the validity of their knowledge—even more so if the daughter is eventually cured by a "healer." The engineering student who succeeds in building the most efficient motor by applying certain principles of physics will have his confidence in those theories confirmed. The church pastor, upon discovering that church leaders live rowdy lives and squander the church's money while preaching the opposite, can experience a crisis of faith and even permanently abandon his religion.

Whether we like it or not, one of the ways we judge the validity of a theory, doctrine, or point of view is by its fruit and its consequences. And this happens from the kitchen to the nuclear physics lab, passing through theology, politics, and bacteriology. What's more, we frequently arrive at condemning, rejecting, or mocking a way of thinking—without knowing it well and without the least amount of study—because the supporters of that vision repeatedly behave in a way that seems contrary to our objectives, values, and expectations.

And, I believe, this is natural: we all want to live the good life as we have been trained to imagine it, and we tend to reject, even without examination, any idea or doctrine that seems to threaten the possibility of fulfilling that dream. Therefore, we sometimes call true that which appears to help us achieve our goals, and false that which looks like a frustrating impediment to our efforts and needs.

Unfortunately, when this happens we can lose a good opportunity to come in contact with other ways of perceiving life and with people who are extremely challenging, innovative, and interesting. What's even worse, this can cause us to underestimate, marginalize, exclude, or persecute—sometimes to the point of elimination—people whose only "defect" is to be different and to think and live in a manner different from our own.

In any case, what I want to suggest is that there is an important and complicated relationship between what we call knowledge (or, more specifically, true and valid knowledge) and the practical experience of power that this knowledge seems to provide. In other words, when we experience that knowledge increases our capacity to achieve what we want, we tend to recognize it as the great truth and as more valid than knowledge that either doesn't affect or negatively affects our power to realize our goals.

The situation of the most oppressed groups in society—for example, those who live with the premature death of loved ones and with their own lives in danger—presents the relation between knowledge and power in a manner that may be more serious and problematic than for other groups. Practical, concrete goals for material survival cannot be underestimated by the oppressed at the moment of determining what is true and what is false. But this definition of what's true and false in the actual life of oppressed people unavoidably enters into conflict with knowledge constructed from the perspective of the powerful.

We see, for example, neoliberal economic theory, which espouses that state intervention in the economy to prevent a rise in unemployment and the deterioration of salaries is an aberration that should be avoided at all costs. (According to the neoliberals' argument, state intervention produces greater ills than the ones we want to correct.) From the perspective of those who do not suffer hunger or homelessness, this theory can seem correct. (After all, for those who have sufficient income, the unemployment and hunger of a few strangers is not nearly as bad as a reduction in their own annual earnings.) Nonetheless, from the point of view of those who suffer low salaries and instability in their work life, neoliberal theory can easily be judged as false. After all, its application will only increase the risk of death for that marginalized person, for his or her family members, friends, colleagues, and neighbors.

In contrast, the most vulnerable members of society, subjected to the interests of a powerful minority, can reject the "truth" that has been imposed on them. After all, such a truth is usually beneficial for the powerful but not for the weakest members of society.

For example, the companies responsible for producing harmful toxins and radioactive waste systematically look for poor communities to offer them money and jobs in exchange for land where they can bury the contaminated waste. In their search, the companies as well as poor communities can produce and interpret all the information within their reach and conclude, for example, that when well handled and buried, the waste doesn't represent any danger whatsoever to human health. For different reasons, both parties can have a clear, practical interest in seeing this opinion as the truth. In the long term, however, it might not only be the most vulnerable but also the most powerful, or their descendants, who become victims for having accepted as "true" what appeared to promise practical, short-term benefits.

I would like to suggest, first of all, that it is dishonest to propose a discussion about knowledge—and the criteria for true knowledge—as though knowing were a purely intellectual, theoretical, contemplative activity, without any relation with the practical, concrete context, goals, and interests of the people who are trying to discern the reality that surrounds them. Generally speaking, this abstract approach to knowledge is typical of intellectuals whose most basic material needs are satisfied and who, deep down, ignore or dismiss those who dedicate most of their waking hours to trying to solve urgent needs of everyday life.

But I want to add that to reduce the problem of truth to a mere relation of knowledge with immediate, practical success is equally deceptive and lazy. It is to forget, among other things, that all success is partial and provisional; that every victory hides an inevitable potential for losing ground and failure; and that in order to be able to serve in the search for the good life, the effort of knowing has to go far beyond the serious and central worries of satisfying our daily longings and desires.

Expanding Our Criteria for Discerning Truth

Philosophers consider many things other than sheer success as criteria for distinguishing true knowledge. But my impression is that many of my philosopher colleagues are too obsessed with finding one single criteria of truth and, furthermore, with seeing the truth as something predominantly intellectual and static.

Allow me, then, to express a few obvious comments and a few consequences. My first comment: until now—and this may be a good thing—no one has been able to resolve the question of what is true knowledge, nor has anyone succeeded in recognizing it in a manner that is clear and satisfying for the entire world or for the majority of specialists in the theory of knowledge. Second, if true knowledge is a theme that deeply touches our interest in living a good life, we cannot leave the answer to a handful of specialists who live far removed from and differently than most people. The consequences? First of all, there is no need to be ashamed—even though we aren't experts—in seriously and frequently interfering in the discussion abut what knowledge and truth are. Second, it's not necessary to let ourselves get carried away with arrogance by the challenge of finding a final solution rather than maintaining the humility to criticize and transform our "solutions" in community, through contact with other perspectives, whether "experts" or not, as well as our own experience, investigations, and creative imagination.

Having said this, I would like to close this part of my reflections by proposing some provocative ideas for reconsider the well-known "criteria of truth" theme.

In the first place, I want to return to some ideas that I suggested in the first chapter of the book and pose them now as questions. Isn't it true that we normally accept what we claim as true knowledge because the whole world does? Isn't it true that there are theories we don't criticize, even though we suspect they are false, for fear of disrespect or persecution? Don't we recognize an opinion as the truth because it's an expert's view, or simply because we feel that we do not know anything about the matter and whoever talks about it sounds so strange that nobody dares discuss it? If these are, even unwittingly, our criteria for truth, the first thing I would propose is to reflect critically on them.

At the same time, I would also encourage us to broaden and multiple our criteria instead of reducing our knowledge to one sole model (e.g., the scientific one). I urge us to recognize and respect many forms and paths of knowing and various types of truth and to value a plurality of ways of understanding, recognizing, and knowing what is "true." Finally, I would propose that we strive to become capable of appreciating, without ranking, the complex differences and relations between distinct "kinds" of knowledge, whether empirical, moral, artistic, technical, mystical, logical, loving, or some other kind.

I would also point out how productive it can be to broaden and deepen our criteria of truth to the point of turning ourselves inside out to see the truth in what's false, and vice versa; to capture that what from a certain perspective is true can be false when viewed from a different angle; how what is true can become false, and vice versa; how *true* and *false* are not exclusive terms without interlocking features and varying degrees and intensity; how what we want to call true and false vary by many factors; and how what we want to call true and false has a lot to do with what we judge in terms of good or bad, just and unjust, or beautiful and ugly. Although the relation may be very complicated, it has a lot to do with our values, priorities, and desires to live a good, festive, and celebratory life.

We could come to imagine what we call true as a collective task, not one of purely personal relevance. Nor would it be simply theoretical or final, like something given once and for all. It would be revisited and reevaluated and always related to the life of people in community—with the traditions, efforts, needs, changes, and creativity of human societies.

The truth can be thought of in relation to the collective reappropriation of knowledge. For example, we might imagine that knowledge would be so much "truer" when deepened and assimilated across the community. Conversely, the more private, secret, and elitist knowledge is, the less true it would become. In this sense, one particular theory—without ever changing a single letter—would become more or less true, according to whether it is reappropriated to a greater or lesser degree by the community.

Likewise, we can think about intellectual autonomy as another criteria of truth: knowledge will be so much "more true," depending on how much it encourages people and communities to think about the reality they share and how much more it frees them to confront, critique, enrich, and creatively transform that knowledge.

The consolidation of the shared good life can be valued as one of the most elevated criteria of truth—even more so today, if we recognize the depth of the challenges that feminism, indigenous rights, ecology, and pacifism present. The more knowledge is compatible with, linked to, and inspired by a community's efforts to nourish and consolidate the good life, for all, the "truer" it is. The more it stimulates solidarity and respect for plurality, diversity, and the rights of minorities, democratic participation, tender treatment of life in all its forms, and enjoyment of the shared life, the more authentic knowledge is. Similarly, when and where knowledge promotes authoritarian attitudes, behaviors, and institutions; racism, machismo, or any other form of discrimination and disrespect against individuals or groups; exploitation or abuse; the violent resolution of disagreements and conflicts; and other initiatives that systematically diminish and destroy personal and community life, the "more false" it is.

Two objections can arise to challenge the proposal of broadening the criteria for truth to the degree I have indicated, and I shall to respond to both. One is that in our actual human communities, where profound conflicts plague different groups, what would be "more true" in one camp would, at the same time, be "less true" for others. The crux of this argument is part of the tragedy of divisions and contemporary social conflicts. That most of humanity aspires to arrive at minimal agreements that permit us to live in peace and harmony indicates that our truths would be more authentic if they were part of a different and better world; if, instead of provoking, sustaining, justifying, and "perfecting" the "arts" of war, domination, and ecological destruction, our truths could help us overcome our difficulties and mend our differences. Said another way, we live in a world so contaminated by falsehood (i.e., the destruction of what is genuinely true, such as life, tenderness, a shared enjoyment of existence), that our poorest and most humble truths could be "really true," could prove and show themselves to be true, only by contributing to the transformation of our world into one that is capable of embracing, stimulating, and nourishing life, tenderness, and solidarity.

This is partly the reason I submit this idea to open discussion. While we continue on the course that we're on, what is designated as "true" by the wealthy and powerful few who control information, education, research, and the means of communication will continue to be affirmed as such by the great majority of people.

No less important is the objection that I mix up and confuse two worlds that should be distinguished and separated: the theoretical-cognitive realm (to which all discussion about knowledge and the criteria of truth pertains) and the practical-ethical realm (which deals with the themes of what is good and bad for life and people). I would respond to this objection in several ways. First, I believe that it is important to distinguish (and not confuse) what is really happening from what could be or ideally should be happening. As I pointed out earlier, we run the risk that our values and interests can cause us to see things incorrectly. Nevertheless, I believe that it is equally interesting to relate (without totally separating) the study of what "really is" with reflection on what "ideally could be"—that is, those values and interests that mark and give meaning to all human life (including knowledge of reality and the concept of truth that we hold). In fact, I would suggest that one of the tragedies of modern philosophy, theology, politics, and science has been the far-too-radical separation of the epistemological problem of knowledge and truth with respect to the ethical problem of goodness and happiness. I would go even further, noting that perhaps this separation is at once a symptom and manifestation of one of the sicknesses of modernity: of being capable of living according to a supposed truth with total indifference to the havoc that our very lives can bring to ourselves, others, and our environment.

Many schools of medicine, law, and economics encourage this lamentable separation by pushing the topic of ethics aside to a few hours a week over the course of one semester. That's it. Consequently, doctors, lawyers, and economists become accustomed to dealing with matters of life and death for others as if "truth" had been established once and for all and there were no further need to reexamine the ethical premises of those very truths.

While recognizing the importance of these and other objections, I'd like to wrap up this discussion by underscoring the need to more intensely reflect on and talk about the connections between our desire for knowledge, especially "true" knowledge, and our wish to live a good life—in community, in peace, and with tenderness, free from violence and oppression.

A BRIEF SYNTHESIS OF THE DISCUSSION

In this chapter, we have revisited a few aspects of the relationship between knowledge and power, placing special emphasis on the connections among knowledge, domination, and the efforts of the oppressed to achieve liberation. As we can see, the situation is complex. We tend to fix our knowledge of reality in simple and solid ideas, and this can help us get our message across and mobilize people. At the same time, we risk that the ruling class will reinterpret our ideas to their advantage or that reality will change, leaving us with an anachronistic vision of our situation.

We need theories to understand and try to transform reality, ranging from the reality of atoms and cells to our economies and religions. Therefore, we commonly end up accepting theories as if they were "the real reality" and refusing to see things in any other way. We become even less inclined to reconsider our views if many people share our theories and if sharing them has brought satisfaction and success.

The role of theories—and their concomitant risks—in the struggle of the oppressed can be appreciated in the process of making enemies and allies. There, theory and reality are interwoven to the point of confusing one with the other.

In collective movements for the transformation of society, there is an acute need for intellectuals—those people and groups who are concentrating on the construction, criticism, and transformation of knowledge.

However, their presence is plagued with ambiguities, and it can be difficult to advance popular movements with their cooperation and involvement. Difficulties arise from the tendency of the nonelites to give the "experts" total control over information and the communication, creation, and transformation of knowledge. And there's always the possibility that experts and intellectuals will use the power handed over to them against the interests of those struggling to overcome oppression.

For these and many other reasons, the oppressed have to place the success of their own liberating efforts as an important criteria in order to discern what should be provisionally accepted as knowledge and what, on the contrary, should be called into question. Clearly, every success is just partial and includes the constant threat of failure. Therefore, it's necessary to look past simple success as the proof of the truth.

Finally, given the complexity of human life and the importance of knowledge, it is worthwhile to think about expanding, multiplying, deepening, and relaxing our criteria of the truth. It's possible that the concept of truth we hold on to—and its radical separation from ethical concerns—is both a symptom of and a factor in the deterioration of human existence in oppressive situations. Once again, I would suggest that reality—and our efforts to know it—is something infinitely richer, more varied, and more complex that we usually believe. Perhaps that is why we have raised many more problems than we've solved in this chapter of the book. Let's continue.

❧ 4. How Do We Express and Share Knowledge?

Let me relate two anecdotes in order to introduce the theme for this chapter.

The first regards the four-decade rule of General Francisco Franco in Spain. Vehemently anticommunist, Franco was a Christian military dictator whose official title was "Leader of Spain by the grace of God." Nonetheless, it was surprisingly possible to publish and sell some Marxist tracts in the final years of his regime. But there were limitations. Not all writers on Marxism were published—only the most difficult to read, like György Lukács, Karel Kosík, and Theodor W. Adorno. Nor were they available at just any price or in any size. The government had abrogated the right to set prices, which made it nearly impossible to find cheap books on Marxism. The government either straight-out prohibited publication of the most compact and accessible texts or made them available only in thick, hefty compilations. In effect, easier-to-read Marxists like Vladimir I. Lenin, Friedrich Engels, Antonio Gramsci, and even Karl Marx himself, didn't exist, or they existed for only a restricted group of well-off individuals and sophisticated intellectuals.

In fact, whoever had trouble reading Castilian Spanish (remember, there are millions of people in Spain who speak other languages, principally Catalan, Basque, and Galician) had only underground access to socialist literature. Although Franco himself was Galician, he directed the systematic repression of the languages and cultures of the Iberian Peninsula other than Castilian. It was impossible to publish about Marxism in Catalan. Nor was it admissible to celebrate a religious service in Galician in Orense, perform a traditional Basque wedding, complete with clothing and dances, in Loyola, or tell stories in Aragonese to schoolchildren in Zaragoza.

The second anecdote I'd like to share concerns a high school classmate in Caracas whose Spanish, both her speaking and writing, was repeatedly corrected by one of our teachers. "Marta," he would reprimand, "That's not how you write it!" or "You always mispronounce *v*, Marta," or "How poorly you speak Spanish, Marta!"

Our teacher was ordinarily a nice man, but one day when Marta seemed especially distressed over her grades, he corrected her once again in front of the whole class: "Child, say your *s*'s. When will you ever learn to speak your own language?" It was the last straw. Marta fled from class in tears and went home.

A few days later, the teacher seemed to have changed his attitude. We asked Marta what happened. "I told my mother," she explained, "who teaches linguistics in the university. She went to talk with our professor and didn't mince any words." "What did she say?" we begged to know. "Hardly anything at all," she continued, "except to say that perhaps he didn't know that Castilian was just one of four languages spoken in Spain and that for centuries it had been looked down upon like bad Latin, spoken by illiterate peasants, and that in Spain, they were revolutionizing Latin. She told him to leave us Venezuelans alone to do the same with his Iberian dialect!"

Nearly all people are born hearing and learning a language, and it becomes so familiar, so spontaneous and unconsciously embedded, that we assume that our language is a natural and everlasting occurrence. Few of us reflect on its history, variety, and changes, and the importance of it all. Unless we have made an effort to know and understand a different culture, with a distinct language, few of us ponder how every language is linked to a particular way of seeing and comprehending the world.

Yet the role of language in shaping and informing our knowledge of reality is precisely the connection I want to underscore. And vice versa: the influence of what we know on our way of speaking to ourselves and to others about the world.

Volumes could be, and have been, written about this very question. I would like to examine only half a dozen examples showing the connection between language and knowledge, especially in relation to several of the problems seriously affecting us today in Latin America.

I'll begin by emphasizing how language simultaneously opens and limits the possibilities of *knowing* reality and taking action to transform it. Next, I will examine how the processes of social domination are frequently accompanied by a kind of "politics of language" aimed at controlling a community's capacity to grasp and change their own reality. Then I will share some reflections on how silence, the apparent *absence* of language, can have completely different meanings in different circumstances. (Thanks to feedback and suggestions from my students in São Paulo, I have added this point to my initial argument.) I will also refer to the efforts of oppressed groups to creatively reappropriate language. In these processes, it is possible to see ways in which liberation is expressed and developed.

When drawing to a close, I will critique elitism and populism, and suggest possible alternatives to this apparent polarization. Finally, I will conclude with some thoughts about important nonverbal languages, such as body language and religious symbolism, and their role in relation to knowledge.

SOME DIMENSIONS OF THIS QUESTION

Language as an Instrument for World Making

Nearly everyone knows that Columbus arrived in the Americas in 1492; that ancient Egyptian pyramids can still be found in the Sahara; that dirty water contains microscopic organisms that can be harmful to human health; and that to physically torture an infant is one of the worst crimes imaginable.

But how do we find out about what happened before we were born? How do we come to know what happened in places we've never been? What investigation have we carried out to inform ourselves of all that we cannot perceive through our senses? Which path do we take to arrive at knowing the norms, beliefs, symbols, and rites that we recognize as valid?

I maintain that most of what we know, we know through language, not through direct personal experience or our own research and investigation. In nearly every instance, we have acquired knowledge through distant or indirect experience that has been communicated to us orally or in writing.

If most of what we know has been transmitted to us rather than experienced firsthand by us, I would dare to say that language is not only our principal tool for the transmission of knowledge. It is also our primary instrument of knowledge. First and foremost, we know the world through the words of others, and only later through our own words, which convey what we see, remember, feel, suspect, know, desire, and dream.

Without language to give voice to it, experience alone remains at the level of personal impression and be hard to convey to others. It's not that impressions are inferior to knowledge or that one can't base knowledge on feelings or intuitions. In fact, an enormous part of what we know is at least partly based on our emotions, and what we feel will really be considered knowledge only if we are able to somehow express it in words.

Language, then, enables us to formulate what we intuit, suspect, discover, or know. It makes it possible for us to relate with other things and advance beyond what we already know. It enables us to reflect, disseminate, confront, and discuss our knowledge.

At the same time, the specific language we use defines possibilities, tendencies, and limits of our knowledge. For example, there are various indigenous languages of Africa, the Americas, Asia, and the Pacific that do not allow mention of the individual as someone separate and distinct from his or her community. Equivalent terms for *I, me, my, with me,* or *mine* do not exist. As a result, the languages themselves compel speakers to think and act like members of a greater whole, always taking into account the rest of the community.[1]

In other indigenous communities, there are languages in which the subject of knowledge is embedded in the grammatical structure. Thus, the mechanics of the language indicate that what someone affirms, he or she knows either firsthand or from another's direct experience. In such languages, it is conceivable to affirm only the things that you yourself, or someone you personally know, have experienced. I call these responsible languages, because it is always clear how the subject knows what he or she knows. However, our modern, "irresponsible" languages allow one to affirm "God exists" or "the economy is in crisis," without making the effort to tell how one came to know such important things.

An old friend told me some interesting things she learned about conversion and community while she was a missionary in Tibet. In Tibetan society, abandoning ancestral religious traditions is something sinful and criminal, whereas converting to another religion can be understood as ascending to a higher level, without ever abandoning the faith of the family. It is difficult for Tibetans to understand the Christian obsession that pushes us to sin against our own community. Nonetheless, many do convert to Christianity but without renouncing their own faith.

For Tibetans, the soul is intimately identified with the idea of seven, as there are seven souls in Tibet. Therefore, they have difficulty grasping the Western Christian notion of saving one's soul. (*Which* soul?) The idea of sin is associated with the rupture of harmony with the cosmos or the community. When Western missionaries arrive preaching that masturbation, for example, is a sin, Tibetans ask, In what way does this destroy cosmic or community harmony? At a loss, the missionaries are unable to provide a satisfactory explanation.

Through language, every culture views, organizes, and *constructs* the world from a perspective that is uniquely theirs and distinct from any other culture or language. Every language defines the possibilities, tendencies, and limits of thoughts as well as actions. For better or worse, this makes it possible or impossible for us to make associations. It pushes us to imagine, desire, or reject some things and not others. It confirms certain behaviors as advisable while prohibiting others as risky or intolerable.

To a profound degree, language marks the possibilities and inclinations of knowing how to act and transform reality.

Domination and Language Control

The importance of language in order to know and transform reality has far-reaching consequences for the power relations among individuals and communities.

When Europeans invaded Africa and America in the fifteenth century, two lucrative industries flourished at the time: the slave trade and the direct exploitation of enslaved Africans. Over the course of four centuries, many millions of Africans, representing hundreds of different cultures and languages, were brought to our America.

Distinct "linguistic policies" appeared in these lands as a result. A common practice among large slave owners who cultivated sugarcane, coffee, or tobacco was to buy slaves from different language backgrounds so that they wouldn't be able to communicate among themselves in a language unknown to their owners. Another was punishing slaves who spoke in their own language and forcing them to speak only in the master's tongue. Still another was prohibiting slaves to learn to read or write. Apart from preventing them from learning things that could be prejudicial against many plantation owners (e.g., the royal or church decrees condemning the widespread practice of physically mutilating rebellious slaves and their accomplices), it made communication among slaves themselves, and protests and mass rebellion, extremely difficult.

Controlling a community's shared language is one of the most effective instruments of domination, and most attempts at domination involve controlling, reducing, and if necessary altogether substituting the language of the oppressed. After that, it is much easier to affect, diminish, or even eliminate the community's capacity to see their predicament as unjust and surmountable. It can reduce the desire and feasibility of taking collective actions to change the status quo.

The Bible is a mixture of sacred writings that have recognized and nourished rebellions against every kind of oppression. Since before Jesus' time, Roman emperors feared unrest from the Jewish population and helped advance a conservative interpretation of Biblical tradition. In large measure, the execution of Jesus and the persecution of the first Christians corresponded to that fear. (Today, accustomed to separating and opposing Jews and Christians, we tend to forget that Jesus and the majority of his earliest followers were Jews.)

When the Emperor Constantine the Great became a Christian two hundred and some odd years later, Christianity became the official religion of the empire, and the leaders of the church passed from the persecuted to the powerful. This gave birth to extremely interesting language policies in relation to the Bible. Church leaders began to define which versions of which ancient Jewish and early Christian texts would be accepted as chosen by God and which would be rejected as apocryphal. Over the course of several centuries, with many conflicts in between, the biblical canon was set, thereby determining the whole of sacred writings for Christian churches.

New language policies were imposed across the Roman Empire as Latin, the language of the literate minority, became the official language of the state and church elites. The canon of the Bible was introduced entirely in Latin and could be transcribed or read only in the official language. As a result, the lower classes of European society did not know any Scripture other than that read and preached from the pulpit by the few priests who could and translate Latin into popular languages. Furthermore, the most innocuous texts and most conservative interpretations often dominated church preaching.

For nearly a millennium, the Christian Church guaranteed what few readings or "subversive" interpretations of Judeo-Christian tradition could be disseminated among those who suffered at the hands of Christian landlords in medieval Europe or in colonial America.

But there are much more subtle ways of exercising control over the language to diminish the possibilities of successful collective rebellions. One is to establish and teach as the "correct language" the way that the elites of a country speak and write the language shared with the masses. To correct, disqualify, mock, or ridicule popular uses of language are part of the politics of linguistics that reinforce, almost unconsciously, the accompanying notion of superiority of the elite minority and the inferiority of the poorer classes. This, of course, consolidates the assumption that those who have greater power and wealth are, in fact, more capable, knowledgeable, and intelligent, and those with less power really are ignorant, uncouth, and lazy. And if they actually do aspire to a better life, they must learn to dress, behave, and speak like the powerful. If they don't conform, they've no right to complain. Therefore, it is important to critically reflect on who is correcting another's use of language, and why, when, where, and with what effects.

Two other habits that can function like linguistic policies for controlling the oppressed deserve mention. One is to use deliberately obscure and confusing language to appear more knowledgeable and thereby consolidate power in a specialized field. Another is to use the language of "experts" when talking with "nonexperts." Both are effective means of silencing the nonspecialist and imposing the interests of the expert over clients, students, or patients. (I am certain that readers will be able to remember concrete experiences of being on one side or the other of the linguistic policies discussed here.)

Communicating in Silence

In order to dominate, ruling classes have a vested interest in silencing the voices of suffering, protest, and denunciation that herald a different world or call others to join in the struggle for a better life. Silencing takes many forms. Complicit silence occurs when we silence what we know to be true, either because we are rewarded or because we fear the consequences of speaking out. Imposed silence may take the form of press censorship, imprisonment, or even genocide. Submissive silence occurs when the oppressed believe the words of the powerful more than they believe in their peers or themselves.

In such cases, it is difficult to construct knowledge of reality that goes beyond the interests and limits imposed by those in power. If successful through repression, propaganda, compensation, or other means, the silencing of the oppressed will signify, at least for a time, a victory for the powerful. It becomes an obstacle that prevents the oppressed from constructing knowledge of reality suited to their traditions, needs, and hopes.

Nonetheless, silence isn't always an obstacle to knowledge or an instrument of oppression. It can be a profound means of communicating experiences, feelings, and knowledge.[2] People who have or remember intimate and long-lasting relationships with others know this well, as do individuals who are unable to communicate through ordinary channels because they are deaf, mute, blind, paralyzed, or partially uncommunicative.

In America, indigenous peoples, African Americans, women, peasants and many other workers have felt forced to cultivate an enormous range of "eloquent silences," especially in relationships with people and groups holding more power.

In several women's prisons in Venezuela, for example, there are windows with grates through which prisoners can extend their hands and see the street. Because official visiting days are few and far between, another kind of visitation from the street has flourished that makes it possible for the prisoners to "speak" with loved ones on the outside. Over time, each inmate and her visitor developed a unique sign language in order to carry on involved, private conversations between the window and the distant street. This shortened the time between official face-to-face visits and made the separation more bearable.

The silence of the listener is indispensable to true communication and essential for the kind of authentic dialogue that actually makes it possible to produce knowledge. Contemplative silence is the capacity of quietly knowing beauty, valor, the sacred, kindness, or simply life itself. Silence can also be an eloquent expression of the demands, hopes, and point of view of the oppressed. Even seemingly docile silence, perhaps accompanied by a slight nodding of the head and an affirmative grumble, can actually mask disagreement and discontent and be well understood by others familiar with the situation as "I don't have the strength right now to resist, maybe later. We'll see."

The glacial silence of defiant or aggressive resistance can announce a storm. The deliberate silence of demonstrators who have gagged their mouths can be a powerful denunciation of censorship of the "forbidden word." Others who fear it would be suicidal to speak out opt for tactical silence and actively, or perhaps patiently, await better times. This silence can go hand in hand with the secret creation of new spaces, means, and forms of communication among the oppressed.

For a Creative Reappropriation of Language

Our relationship with language is simultaneously a symptom of and a support for our links with reality, including our method of knowing what's real. We can take a rigid and submissive stance, thinking that each word has a single, clear, and permanent meaning, and that dictionaries and know-it-alls are there to teach us the definitive meaning and use of language.

Such an attitude generally coincides with a hierarchical and authoritarian conception of reality in which all people and things have their exclusive and inalterable place; in which the inferior always yield to their superior; and in which if we learn the one correct way of knowing from the experts, we will reach the one and only immutable truth.

I remember a brief but difficult exchange that took place in 1971 between two Latin American students in Europe. Elena and Ángel were debating the usefulness of a multiparty democratic system. Ángel argued, "In *The State and the Revolution*, Lenin says . . . " Elena interrupted him, demanding, "Stop! I want to know what *you* think, not Lenin!" This little encounter illustrates that instead of using our own heads, we often turn to others and quote their words for a definitive answers to our concerns.

Of course, this isn't merely a way of looking at language, reality, and knowledge. This rigid and docile way of positioning ourselves is counterproductive for anyone who wishes to transform reality and improve oppressive social relationships.

Speech and every language can be viewed as human creations in a permanent state of flux, full of the complexities and tensions that form part of life. Language can be understood as a dynamic ensemble of tools for expressing, communicating, and transforming human experience. Furthermore, we can understand it as a dimension of community life, finely interwoven with other aspects of life, which simultaneously demands, enables, and limits the creative participation of everyone who shares the same language.

If we understand language as a dynamic and participatory phenomenon, it will be easier to integrate it into the productive, liberating efforts aimed at transforming our lives.[3]

To actively and collectively participate in the creative reappropriation of shared language can promote our capacity to know reality anew in the context oppression we seek to change.

Let's look at a couple of historical examples to illustrate this point.

When European empires invaded America in the fifteenth and sixteenth centuries, the Protestant Reformation was progressing in Europe. One of the great changes introduced by the Reformation—as the printing press was spreading—was the translation of the Bible into German, French, English, and other popular European languages. For the first time in a thousand years, this put the entire Bible within the reach of many listeners. Given that few people could read, many preachers read aloud, in "vulgar" languages, biblical texts that were previously unknown. Within a few years, thousands of peasants appropriated biblical language as the foundation and symbol of their hopes for a better life, and they rose up in the so-called Anabaptist Peasants' War in Germany and Bohemia against the landlords who had been exploiting them for generations.

The Sandinista Revolution in Nicaragua, from 1979 to 1991, can be viewed as a creative reappropriation of a shared language. In this case, the language derived from socialist, democratic, Christian, and Sandinista traditions, in the particular Spanish of this Central American country. In a few years, the Sandinista Front succeeded in creating an original platform that articulated many fundamental aspirations of the Nicaraguan people in the 1980s. They were able to express them with important elements of the four traditions mentioned earlier and to criticize aspects of those traditions that were repugnant to the Nicaraguan people and international public opinion. Finally, they were able to express this collection of ideas in a language and in original forms of communication authentic to the majority of Nicaraguans. With their platform, the Sandinista Front contributed to a successful mobilization, first against the Anastasio Somoza dictatorship and then in favor of a participatory, pluralistic democracy with a mixed and more autonomous economy.

I would call these creative reappropriations of a shared language of the oppressed: biblical language of German and Bohemian peasants in the fifteenth and sixteenth centuries, in one case, and in the other, Nicaraguan-style popular political-religious Spanish of the 1970s to 1990s in the twentieth century.[4]

The reappropriation of language on the part of the oppressed could be simply understood as "learning." The right-wing view holds that the poor are poor because they haven't had adequate education to climb the ranks of the society, whereas the left-wing explanation faults the poor for failing to rise up against the system. In either case, the emphasis is on *learning* as something preexisting, something taught by *others*, namely, those who "already know."

But I want to suggest an alternative view: knowledge is always to be made, remade, critiqued, and transformed, and language is one of the principal instruments of constructing, communicating, criticizing, and transforming knowledge. To deliberately transform reality in accordance with the values and goals shared by a community, it is necessary to simultaneously transform our vision of the world along with the language with which we express it. However, if we passively and submissively limit ourselves to preexisting knowledge and language, it will be difficult to contribute to the transformation of our reality beyond the framework of the dominant values of our society.

Therefore, if we seek to improve oppressive relationships, we have to reclaim the language we have inherited from the past and the ideas expressed therein and increasingly take possession of that newly reclaimed language. We must collectively critique it, creatively transform and enrich it, until we are able to independently see and articulate our experience of oppression and express our hope for liberation.

Then the creative reappropriation of language by those who suffer from oppression becomes a fundamental liberating task.

Marginalization, Liberation, and Language
Surely everyone who reads these lines has heard and read expressions like "murky waters" and "clear waters." Likewise, we are familiar with rebukes and insults like "He must be an Indian!" and an endless variety of jokes ridiculing indigenous people and African Americans. Similarly, people make insults and jokes at the expense of sectors of society with little power and

appreciation from elites: peasants, women, homosexuals, workers, residents of ghettos and slums, people who live outside of the capital, immigrant workers, people with disabilities, the elderly, and the illiterate.

It is hard to find similar taunts about powerful groups, but those we do find invariably ridicule members of elite sectors for being "tainted" because of some characteristic, relative, or ancestor who is linked to less powerful groups of society.

These are the ways we use language to express and consolidate, often unconsciously, the relationships of domination that characterize our societies.

The vast majority of human communities have lived for generations under the thumb of other sectors of society. Oppression habitually marks the language and it surfaces in the jokes, insults, praises, and other emotionally charged expressions of the community, even in compliments and professions of love. The power dynamics of the community not only reverberate throughout the language. The social arrangement between the rich and the poor, the powerful and powerless, the oppressed and the oppressor—this is a principal source of meaning of the language itself.[5] Because of all this, struggles for self-esteem, emancipation, and autonomy are fought in the territory of language.

In effect, we could affirm that language plays a key role in the process of liberation. If our way of talking about reality, our speech, stays the same as it is expressed under oppressive conditions, language will reinforce a conservative vision of reality. Consequently, our way of responding to reality will tend to confirm and consolidate the oppressive conditions we want to alter, despite our intentions to the contrary. Most critics of racism, sexism, classism, and other isms that plague our daily speech share this hypothesis.

In contrast, we could constantly attempt—in community—a critique and transformation of everyday language, with the goal of expressing a more open, flexible, humble, and egalitarian vision of humanity. Such an effort, if it is persistent and collective, can contribute to spreading, deepening, and expanding this very same vision of reality. In the midst of this dynamic, it is much more probable that practical initiatives aimed at changing reality will flourish.

In this sense, I would suggest that the freeing of language could be effective in any liberation effort, especially if what is sought is to construct, discuss, communicate, criticize, and modify knowledge of reality in order to transform it.

Common-Folk Language: Elitist versus Populist Assessments

I recall an experience I had when I first starting coming to the United States, as a guest lecturer invited by various Latino groups. From my earliest talks, all related to the themes discussed in this book, I could tell that some people in the audience did not understand what I was trying to say. At first I thought it was a question of language, so I explained my ideas in Spanish and in English, but some people remained confused. Fearing I was talking above their heads, I tried a clearer, simpler, and more orderly approach using examples, jokes, and some drawings and diagrams on the blackboard. Things got better for some but not everyone.

The strange thing is that this had never happened before with Latinos in Latin America or with native English speakers in the States. Therefore, I spent several intense days talking it over with Latinos and leaders of the institution that sponsored my talks.

As time went on, I began to understand that part of the problem stemmed from the fact that many of the people in attendance were illiterate in Spanish. It was the language spoken only at home and undervalued by the outside world, including the church, school, the military, and police, offices, businesses, and employers. It was even underappreciated in some Latino homes, where families were desperate to adapt and succeed in the United States.

With the exception of people who never went to school because they worked since childhood, nearly everyone who had difficulty with my talks normally spoke, read, and wrote in English. Nevertheless, English represented an *imposed language*: the foreign language required by the school, the army, the job, the business world, and television. Neither in the undervalued Spanish of the home and childhood nor in the strange, arrogant, cold English forced upon them did anyone have the experience of discussing politics, theology, or social, ethical, or philosophical problems.

As a result, the world of language and knowledge was far removed from the majority of the Latinos in attendance and a good percentage of the people who grew up speaking English at home.

In a situation like this, how could I stimulate a critical reappropriation or a certain liberation of language? Even though I do not have the answer, it seems crucial to start from the real, authentic language of the oppressed as they speak, write, read, and understand it.

I suppose we could start from the language of the elites or a particular slang from certain "critical minorities," such as existential philosophers, theologians of liberation, socialist politicians, feminist writers, Afrocentric historians, Marxist sociologists, or indigenous anthropologists. In fact, I believe that this is what is most commonly done.

But I think that this can aggravate the situation and unintentionally confirm what most marginalized people hear everyday in every aspect of their lives: that they do not know how to speak, understand, or change their own reality; it is others who speak correctly, adequately understand reality, and are capable of transforming it; the powerless are ignorant, brutish, and incapable and they should passively and docilely leave it to the elites, whether they are leftist, centrist, or right-wing; professionals, politicians, economists, or religious; atheists, Muslims, Catholics, Jews, or Protestants.

I would liberating politicians of this stripe elitist, not because they came from wealthy sectors of society or were educated by their patrons, but because they conform to the prejudice that only a select few know what "the masses" should say, think, and do. As I see it, this prejudice encourages passivity, submission, and self-destruction among the marginalized at the same time that it consolidates the power, attitudes, and behavior of the elites and keeps oppressive conditions in tact.

Therefore, I reiterate my earlier point that a specific liberation of language must emerge from the actual language that is spoken, written, read, and understood by the oppressed.

Nonetheless, there is another tendency, populism, that seems interesting to analyze as we consider efforts to free language. I would define populism as a frank, noncritical validation of what it is, quite simply, popular. Frequently crafted by the elites, populism can also be useful in fomenting a superficial harmony between the powerful minority and the masses without changing the oppressive relations between them.

Oftentimes, the real and authentic language of the oppressed is profoundly marked by oppression itself. Developed under the influence of the elites, popular language is full of mechanisms for imitating and adapting dominant values. In many ways, the language itself is a vehicle of oppression and often oozes resentment and self-loathing. In addition, it is frequently "impoverished" in that it lacks the information, technological, and cultural terminology and expressions capable of conveying the reality that only the elites continually and constantly access.

I believe that investigating, recuperating, valuing, vindicating, and spreading the language of the "masses" are means of overcoming our elitist tendencies. But *getting stuck* there is to forget and reinforce the idea that everyday language is, at least partially, both an instrument of the processes of social domination and the fruit the material and spiritual expropriation that often leaves the oppressed without resources to expand, enrich, criticize, or remake their world. Real and authentic language of the oppressed often presents obstacles to grasping, expressing, and communicating the dynamic complexity of reality. At the same time, the language, whatever it is, is usually insufficient to nurture the critical and transformative capacity of marginalized sectors of society.

But as they investigate, recuperate, value, vindicate, and spread popular language, perhaps the oppressed themselves could undertake a collective task that includes critical analysis and the creative transformation of everyday language.

But I don't think this is enough. The language of the elites also has to be taken into account. It isn't only an instrument of domination in the hands of the powerful; it is also a tool of expression, communication, and control of the reality they know and rule. This is exactly what makes the language of the elites an instrument of domination. Subsequently, it becomes the norm in the education system, the criteria for social and professional selection, and a common reference among those who speak the same language, albeit differently.

Everyday and elitist languages are essentially dialects of the same language. To rule better, the elites not only need to know their own dialect. They also need intellectuals who are versed in everyday, popular language and have the capacity and willingness to transmit the values and interests of the elites to the masses in their dialect.

Equally, to better resist domination and to increase the possibilities of success in their efforts to transform that situation of domination, the masses *also* need the language of the elites. Any poor child who has finished primary school or experienced the power of elitist language knows this. In general, this knowledge is relayed, and takes hold, upon learning to speak and write like the rich in order to be able to individually succeed in life. Very often, a child ends up forgetting and despising his or her own language.

It seems necessary to go further and become socially bilingual: to creatively and critically reappropriate one's own language, become a proud owner of it, and develop all of its liberating potential. At the same time, it is important to know how to use the dominant dialect as a kind of second language and a tool for transformation.

Beyond the Written Word

Don't most political discussions tire you out? What about religious sermons and leftist pamphlets? And economic analyses in most newspapers? It's not a matter of not understanding. Sometimes these tracts and sermons are written in clear, everyday language. It's not even that they are full of lies or of little importance. They often bring truthful and serious information. But don't they lack humor, love, affection, a sense of humanity, and reality? Don't they seem to be missing variety, color, imagination, and real life?

I believe that a large part of the difficulty with discourse is that it relies too heavily on the spoken word, prose, intellectual abstractions, cold facts, and logical reasoning as the superior and privileged vehicles of knowledge. But these vehicles for imparting knowledge are not only the dialect of a particular tribe. The greater problem is that this "particular tribe" is more closely linked to the powerful than the marginalized. Frequently taking on the airs and styles of the privileged, this contributes to regarding the jargon of specialists, experts, and intellectuals as the best language for communicating, discussing, and reconstructing human knowledge.

On the other hand, are you familiar with the music of Mercedes Sosa, Chico Buarque, Rubén Blades, Juan Luis Guerra and 440? Or the cartoons of Quino, Zapata, or Gila? And what do you think of Gioconda Belli's poetry, the novels of Rubem Fonseca, the meditations of Don Hélder Câmara, Oliver Stone's films, Marina Colasanti's articles, and Alice Walker's book? Don't they all contain knowledge, a fondness for investigation, recovered history, clarification of theories, criticism of dominant proofs, and even epistemological vigilance and ruptures, and all that with greater frequency than we find in the verbosity of many of our experts?

Human languages—and the forms of expressing, communicating, criticizing, and transforming knowledge—are infinitely richer and varied than verbal prose and wordy discourse. There's poetry, sonnets, myth, song, maxim, impulse, metaphor, parable, rap, anecdote, story, prayer, joke, meditation, fable, irony, satire—and countless ways of using these. In addition, there are many other languages and forms of expression and communication that can also serve to spread, evaluate, and transmit our knowledge, such as theater, puppetry, feast, religious symbolism, dance, music, caricature, painting, sculpture, touch, gestures, a look, and endless combinations of all of the above!

For me, the liberation of language is the thousands of actual efforts at reconstructing and multiplying languages that arise from oppressive realities into languages that are capable of heralding new ways of living that are open, flexible, humble, pluralistic, brotherly, egalitarian, participatory, and cooperative. Freeing language goes far beyond abstract intellectual exercises with verbal prose. It happens not only with the word in all of its diversity, but beyond, in the most varied settings and the most diverse channels where we try to connect with one another, express ourselves, love and know one another. That's where we are going to enjoy, celebrate, heal, nourish, multiply, defend, protect, communicate, and—in community with one another—give meaning to our lives.

A genuine liberation of popular languages from the world of the oppressed passes through many of the forms of sharing, criticizing, and enriching the awareness shared among ordinary people. When they are liberating, these efforts help unfasten the chains that relegate the speech, experience, and wisdom of ordinary people to a subordinate and unappreciated status within our communities. They can also build bridges, though tense and problematic, for authentic dialogue between the base and the most diverse specialists. Hopefully, many essays on liberation written in popular language become nourishment in the life of marginalized communities of our America.

A BASIC SYNTHESIS OF THE DISCUSSION

Whether or not we realize it, we know our reality through the language we inherited from past generations and continually acquire from the people with whom we live. Although we do not always realize it, our language serves as a tool for comprehending the surrounding world. It is an instrument of expression, transmission, discussion, critique, and transformation of the knowledge we create in community.

Just as language makes knowledge possible, it also orients and imposes limits on knowledge. There are things we don't know how to say, even though we experience them profoundly, or that we are incapable of grasping because of the limitations of language. Some things we pay close attention to because our language takes us there, just as there are things that are possible because we have language that reflects our experience.

When one group tries to dominate another, language immediately comes into play to justify, question, hide, or denounce the violence under way. If attempts at subjugation are successful for several generations, our own ways of seeing and speaking about reality will become so transformed that they tend to express and confirm that victory.

Consequently, the resistance to domination and the impulse to free oneself or one's community become intimately bound to a language that is shared. In part the fruit of resistance, but also marked by the very same domination, language is necessary preparation for as well as a potential obstacle to the ability of the marginalized to perceive, tell, discuss, and transform their living conditions.

Therefore, I refer to the liberation of language as the desire felt in many Latin American communities today to recuperate, deepen, and reflect on the forms of expression of the oppressed—their ways of defining, telling, remembering, supporting, hiding, resisting, crying, meditating, ridiculing, denouncing, praising, rejoicing, announcing, and celebrating life.

But that's not all. The liberation of language can also include all attempts within and outside of oppressed communities to detect and overcome all of the oppressive characteristics of actual language, to fuel and reaffirm attitudes, relationships, and behaviors that are violent, authoritarian, abusive, discriminatory, and destructive.

Perhaps we'll someday be able to see and speak of reality in such a way that inspires peace, justice, and tenderness.

⌖ 5. Rethinking Our Understanding of Knowledge

In the 1980s, when Ronald Reagan was president of the United States, a minor scandal stirred up the press and political world: serious economic, political, and military decisions of the most powerful government on the planet were made by Reagan after consultation with close friend of the First Lady and astrologist Jeane Dixon. Friends and advisers of the president both confirmed and denied the reports, some refused to comment, and others simply affirmed that confusion reigned in the White House. Dixon herself saw her book sales and contracts increase, while newspapers and magazines the world round filed reports on similar occurrences in many current and past governments.

More than thirty years ago, I read a *Life* magazine article on Haiti. The reporter related his visit with a working woman in the capital, Port-au-Prince. At a certain moment in the interview, the woman excused herself for a few minutes, went out to the patio, and stood with her hands on the trunk of a tree. Upon returning, the reporter asked her what was going on. The woman replied that her husband had gone to the market on errands, and she had forgotten to ask him to pick up a few things. So she went to the tree, she explained as a matter of fact, because they did not have a telephone.

Naturally, the journalist extended the interview until the woman's husband returned—with the very things his wife had mentioned.

• • •

Whenever the subject of human knowledge comes up, many questions arise, such as, can't we be certain about anything? What if scientific knowledge isn't verifiable, irrefutable, and in constant progress? Where does truth reside? Is everything really relative, equal, and right? And what about error and lies? What's the relation between scientific knowledge and other forms of knowledge?

In this final chapter on human knowledge and its relation to the transformation of unjust social conditions, I am going to quickly touch upon some crucial questions.

Before proceeding, I want to reiterate that I neither claim to nor want to exhaust this subject in all of its possible facets. What I do aim to do is touch upon some the most serious and urgent aspects of the problem of knowledge in the Americas today.

I would also like to make it equally clear that I don't have the last word on the subject. I would merely like to propose some provocative ideas to stimulate questioning, open-mindedness, pluralism, curiosity, research, critical reflection, discussion, and creative imagination. In fact, I am convinced that there is a shortage of these very things. But there is an abundance of unreflective certainties, close-mindedness, dogmatism, fear of venturing into unknown territory, passivity, conformity, and the incapacity to discuss these things in a serious, intense, and extensive way. Especially in these years of crisis, paralyzing doubts, self-destructive uncertainties, confusion, chaos, resignation, indecision, and fear abound.

Having said this, we are going to examine a set of problems that seem too important to leave out of the reflections shared here. Some were raised in earlier chapters but will be more fully developed here.

First is the question of science, truth, progress, and scientific methods. Then we will refer to the role of emotions and feelings in human knowledge and their relation to reason. Further along, we will touch upon the subject of activity and relativity of knowledge. Next, we will examine various proposals for thinking about knowledge in a slightly uncommon way: knowledge of that which doesn't exist, prejudice (knowledge gained prior to actual experience), recognition (remembering something previously experienced), cognition (a collective task), and finally, ignorance (active and sometimes necessary ignorance).

After visiting these thorny issues, we'll jump into other equally difficult questions. We'll penetrate the reasons knowledge is always undergoing transformation. We will talk about the difficulties of maintaining a conception of the truth as something absolute, universal, permanent, and wholly unique, and also consider some alternatives. Then we'll deal with the separation between knowledge and reality, the individual and the whole, and subjectivity and objectivity. While these distinctions may be useful, they are artificial, and it is important to see them as constructions we've created. We will close the discussion by proposing an understanding of knowledge as a fragmented, partial, imaginative, and provisional reconstruction of reality.

Once again, we remain well aware of the fact that there is much more to be said than we have said, that we have also proposed more problems than we've resolved, and that things can be more confusing than they appeared at the onset. I hope that this provokes new questions, searches, discussions, and ways of looking at reality.

SOME DIMENSIONS OF THIS QUESTION

Modern Sciences: Usefulness or Idolatry?

Prior to the eighteenth century, certain forms of knowledge became increasingly popular in Europe and began to be regarded as superior to all the rest. It was as if they held the key to all that religion had promised but postponed until the "afterlife," namely, human liberty and happiness.

These forms of knowledge draw heavily from a variety of sources including mathematics developed by the Arabs; alchemy from medieval Europe; philosophical traditions of the Chinese, the British, and the Greeks; the anticlerical attitudes and faith in the power of human reasoning that were especially pronounced in Europe during the French Revolution; and the liberal bourgeoisie's general optimism about the inevitable progress of humanity toward greater reason, liberty, and happiness.

Starting back in eighteenth-century Europe, the mix of these disparate elements gave an energetic push to scientific experimentation; the miniscule observation of reality (aided by the construction and use of telescopes and microscopes); the invention of the steam engine, industrial looms, and other complex tools used in production; the development of new theories about the cosmos, matter, and life (e.g., Newton's laws of physics, Lavoisier's discoveries about chemistry, and Darwin's theory of evolution); and the application of calculus—then regarded as absolutely rational and infallible—to all of these activities.

In Europe before the 1600s, these works were usually considered part of philosophy, theology, medicine, military arts, or, to put it more simply, of human labor. Little by little, however, universities and the press began to give more attention and place more trust in these tasks. New, relatively independent forms of knowledge such as astronomy, geology, physics, and biology developed slowly but surely, as certain contours, themes, jargon, methods, goals, books, specialists, useful applications, prestige, and awards emerged to distinguish them.

Until the past few centuries, the common language of the intellectual class was Latin. In Latin, *scire* means "to know." From there the word *scientia*, meaning "the known things," emerged and gave birth to the word *science* in English (and to similar terms in other languages).

Like all words, the word *science* has a history, and its meaning has varied over the centuries. Even in the nineteenth century, *science* simply meant knowledge, awareness, things known and recognized.[1] But *science* has come to signify those specific forms of knowledge cited already that began to acquire prestige and independence in Europe in the 1700s.

Of all these modern sciences, physics became the model, the norm, the prototype. There is still a tendency today to consider a discipline much more scientific when it most resembles physics.

And just what are the characteristics of physics? The truth is that it depends on the specialist who is asked. Nonetheless, many agree that the following attributes are key characteristics of a modern science: clear definitions of the terms that are used preferably in reference to observable data and mathematically expressible relations, repeated experimentation that can be shared with and repeated by other specialists, use of the most precise instruments possible for quantitative measurement of the elements implicated in the experiment, mathematic formulation of the results of the experimental investigation, construction of theories capable of predicting future behaviors of analogous realities, and the like.

These rules of the game habitually used by physicists are often called the scientific method. Disciplines that exhibit a certain similarity and interaction with physics commonly fall under the name *Science*.

Nonetheless, science, in the singular, has never existed. But there are sciences, in the plural: varied disciplines with their own unique histories, specialists, universities and schools, texts, awards, theories, magazines, vocabulary, and discussions. These disciplines are seen in relation to and in conflict with other sciences, scientific methods, and forms of knowledge.

Nor has the scientific method existed. There are rules, notions, techniques, and guidelines that emerge and enter into conflict with other disciplines.[2] They are gradually and partially imposed and then end up becoming "normal and accepted" with the passage of time. As the physicist, mathematician, and historian of science Paul Feyerabend has noted, the great discoveries, inventions, and changes in the history of the sciences have generally resulted from critically revising and improving—that is, from transgressing the scientific methods until they are accepted and consecrated in a given epoch, discipline, and region.[3]

Throughout their history, the sciences and the scientific method have stimulated careful attention to what has really occurred around us, independent of our conscious intentions, beliefs, and feelings. They have encouraged a tendency for systematic observation, with repeated experimentation under similar and different conditions, as a means of assuring ourselves of the validity of our conclusions. They have also forged a deliberate opening for discussion, critical reflection, and revision of the findings of our investigations. It seems to me that all these characteristics should be valued and taken advantage of to improve the conditions of human existence in our actual world.

The sciences are extraordinarily useful and important in the world today. Directly or indirectly, the economic, political, sanitation, military, educational, and communications wherewithal—the very underpinnings of life and death—depends on scientific production, as do the chances of our longings for a lasting justice and peace.

Whereas these facts alone might be enough to convince ourselves that the sciences should be taken seriously, I believe that they must be placed in the service of every effort made to transform society.

These facts should not blind us to another key consideration: what some call science and what I would call the worship of science. I am referring to the naive yet widely disseminated and accepted attitude that the only valid knowledge is scientific fact. Supposedly it is universal, accumulative, permanent, and absolutely true and good. Accordingly, such knowledge can be controlled and judged only by scientists themselves, not by laypeople or even democratically elected representatives.

Such idolatry presumes a bias favoring Newtonian physics in model and scientific criteria, whether it is true and worthy of attention and value. According to this perspective, the human sciences such as sociology, anthropology, and psychology are "subsciences" with less validity. In this line of thinking, each science should focus on its particular object (with its methods, vocabulary, and specialists) without getting involved in other camps or allowing outsiders in. To make matters worse, such fragmentary specialization leaves no place for nonscientific ethical, ecological, social, religious, and political concerns.

Worship of science worries me for two reasons. First, this is the image of science that is divulged by most of schools, means of communication, businesses, and armies I know of, regardless of political orientation. Second, I believe that this perception discourages people from questioning the important role of science in weapons manufacturing, ecological destruction, and the growing misery and violence endemic in the world.

What's tragic, I think, is that while many scientists are redoubling their efforts and resources to save, heal, and help human life, an increasing share of the world's scientific experts, tools, money, education, and research is dedicated to sustaining and defending the economic adventures and life-styles of a small wealthy minority from the most powerful countries on the planet.

The sciences are a recent human creation, more and more decisive as regards who, how, when, and where we are going to live and die. All human beings, whether specialists or laypeople, have the need and the right to intervene in a deliberate, organized, ongoing, and critical way in the activities, including the scientific, that affect the quality of our lives and our deaths. This is especially true today, as vested financial and military interests are turning the sciences into destructive weapons in the hands of powerful elites rather than into tools at the service of the vast majority of the human family.

Reason, Emotions, and Knowledge

YZ was a militant dedicated to the struggle for social change in Latin American. He was an old and much loved friend of many people I know. When he was taken prisoner in the 1970s, he gained the deepest admiration of fellow prisoners, the party itself, and even a number of politicians for having endured prolonged and unspeakable tortures without breaking or betraying anyone. Neither the pain nor the terror he experienced were able to crush his spirit or his principles. After surviving his nightmarish ordeal, he was eventually treated better and permitted visits from his wife and others.

One day he found out that his wife was living with another member of the party. Devastated and bewildered, he called the secret police and revealed everything he had withheld during his torture. As a result, a comrade was forced underground, imprisoned, tortured, and eventually killed.

Human emotions, often unexpected and unpredictable, can distort our perception of reality as well as our values, principles, customs and ability to reason, especially in traumatic situations. How else can we begin to explain the rebirth of Nazism in so many countries at the end of the twentieth century?

A tragic aspect of idolizing science can produce an exaggerated confidence in human reason, as if the ability to examine facts in a cold, logical, and objective manner would reveal the meaning of human existence and point the way to the good life. Unfortunately, things aren't so simple. Human reason isn't so powerful, believable, or independent of other dimensions of existence, despite what even the most intolerant rationalists would have us believe. It doesn't exist in the abstract or in a vacuum far removed from a tangible social reality. Different cultures, at different times, enjoy the capacity to reflect, draw conclusions, pose and resolve problems, and organize various means to achieve certain ends. In each and every culture, the way of understanding "reason" varies and changes under an endless number of influences.

This does not mean that reason is bad and should be entirely done away with. Like many indispensable medicines, reason must be taken with care, in moderation, and accompanied by other elements. Otherwise its isolated and exaggerated use can be toxic to health. It can be as harmful as an overdose of pure sentimentalism, intuition, or irrationalism.

It seems to me that most of the truly important decisions we make in life are not solely based on rational thought. In moments of greatest happiness, as in life's most tragic situations, reason alone serves us very little. We repeatedly experience that personal relations, traditions, emotions, and beliefs count more and often find ourselves espousing views and living in ways that are radically opposite from the dictates of reason. How we feel, think, and act is conditioned by our emotional experiences in life, above all during childhood.

We have discussed this in the section of the book concerned with how experience shapes and influences our knowledge. Now I want to zero in on reason and its relation to our emotional and sentimental lives. Let me be very clear. I am not trying to add to the destructive irrationalist way of discrediting or attacking reason. My aim is to situate reason in a more global and balanced perspective in relation to knowledge, community, and the individual.

On the one hand, we have the rational capacity, both personal and collective, to go beyond our particular circumstances, to put some distance between our own thoughts and emotions, to critically analyze our behavior, to see things from another perspective, and to humbly enter into a dialogue with people who see things differently. We are able to break the deceptive veil of tradition and consensus and compare, suspect, evaluate, and draw conclusions. That ability is useful in order to get out of irrational jams when fear, attraction, anger, or custom leads us to behaviors that are destructive and contrary to our own values, interests, and ideas.

On the other hand, relations, feelings, values, norms, and interests are fundamental dimensions of human existence, and they often override reason. Concerned with profound bonds of family, love, community, country, religion, ethnicity, and language, they can be the source of knowledge that is difficult to access solely through reason. Keep in mind the French adage of Blaise Pascal, "The heart has reasons that reason cannot know."

For example, a community's struggle to hold onto its land that others might wish to exploit for underground uranium mining can seem irrational from the perspective of a private company that wants to explore the territory and or from the angle of a state interested in increasing its national mineral wealth. Viewed by a group of scientists wanting resources for experimentation in nuclear physics or from the perspective of unemployed workers from a neighboring city who are anxious about finding jobs, it may seem absurd. But for a community threatened by displacement, this struggle to keep their land can be one of life and death, and it demands recognition and respect from powers outside of the community.

Struggles within economic, political, religious, or labor organizations that comprise peasants, indigenous people, or other oppressed groups frequently occur when their bonds, relationships, and needs come into conflict with the supposedly rational demands of the more powerful. Such dimensions and relationships are not necessarily irrational, contrary, or unreasonable. Not at all. They are frequently examined, critically evaluated, and heavily influenced by our capacity to reason. But as Marx, Nietzsche, and Freud suggest, human reason is always ready to rationalize or justify actions on the basis of emotions, affection, and self-interests like personal wealth, fame, power, and electoral victory. It's just as evident in individuals and movements that present themselves as altruistic and dedicated to higher causes.

This has contributed to a cynical irrational individualism that insists, "Everything I want and can do is valid, and no one has the right to ask me for explanations." In such instances, reason must respond by pointing out that our entire life is possible only because of the work of others with whom we have communication, bonds, and irrefutable ethical responsibility. Of course, our values, loyalties, feelings, and interests will contribute to directing and stimulating the capacity to examine our lives. Hopefully, we will enter into a fertile and reciprocal exchange in which our deepest bonds and feelings inspire us to reason and our ability to think critically contributes to improving the dynamics that lead us to destruction.

Knowledge as Imaginative Reconstruction of Relationships

As an experiment, let us take something we are very familiar with, such as a plant, and analyze it to try to know it inside and out. When we do this, our attention turns to an isolated feature. We zero in on the sizes, shapes, and colors. We sense the smells, tastes, and tactile sensations. We imagine its origins, processes, and results. We classify, compare, remember, associate, and disassociate. Whether or not we realize it, our capacity to imagine relations comes into full play when we undertake so simple as exercise as identifying a plant.

Very often, knowing is understood as the passive capacity to appropriately capture isolated information. An interesting medieval theory influenced by the earlier thought of Aristotle defines knowledge as an adaptation from the mind to the object. A more recent theory of Lenin regards knowledge as a mental reflection of reality.

I would like to propose the possibility of conceiving knowledge as relative imagination. Rather than the passive capacity to capture things in isolation, to know is the particular ability to intervene in reality by imagining relationships among elements that emerge from collective and individual experience.[4] Knowledge affects reality, testing the point to which these relationships are capable of taking real experience into account.

Furthermore, we could think of independent things as links on a chain of relationships in which we are actively involved, thus making it possible for us to grasp and compelling our interest in knowing them. Our connections with reality are in a constant state of flux. Things are not mere objects separated from one another and from us. They are tied to us, and it's as a part of this dynamic network that we try to creatively imagine how these links emerge and change. It is also where we check out whether our theories are interesting, fertile, or beneficial.

We share the desire to know reality in a global, universal, radical, and definitive way. Perhaps this aspiration is what pushes us to go beyond where we have already arrived, to not satisfy ourselves with what we suspect is partial, provisional, and presumptuous. This impetus stirs an investigative desire and intellectual creativity in humanity. Unfortunately, we sometimes believe that we have arrived at global, universal, radical, and definitive knowledge (and that whoever thinks differently is wrong and should be educated, converted, restricted, punished, or eliminated).

Mindful of these possible consequences, it is more important than ever to be aware that knowledge is not finite and definitive; that the variety, richness, and metamorphosis of reality are infinite and inexhaustible; that the human capacity to know is diverse, exuberant, and immense; that what is to be learned is absolutely more vast and important that what we can teach; that knowledge is part of life, and like life, it stops (and perhaps just on the surface) only upon death.

It is not easy to think in these terms when everyday experience usually points us in a very different direction (toward "things" that are outside of our relationships; where knowing is to see things as they are, without modification; and where truth is the correct and immutable description of the way things are). But this book is an attempt to think about knowledge as dynamic, open, relative, critical, and creative.

In truth, discussions like the one we are having here often give rise to the sometimes fearful, sometimes accusatory challenge: "Aha! So everything is relative!" I believe that this is so, if by *relative* we mean not isolated, absolute, or just living for one's self. If we agree that nothing exists in isolation, that everything is linked, then, yes, everything is relative. I would add that all knowledge emerges from experience and the practice in which we are connected to our surroundings and to ourselves and that knowing implies imagining ties between diverse elements of our experience. All knowledge can conjure new connections and be questioned and transformed from other relationships. Consequently, even if we isolate ourselves from the rest of the universe in the pursuit of knowledge, neither what we know is really separate nor does our knowledge develop in a vacuum. In this sense, I would say that all knowledge is indeed relative!

If we understand *relative* to mean false, illusory, deceptive, or indifferent, I cannot accept that everything is relative. For the community in the midst of a drought, for example, that imagines and tests possibilities for finding water in a certain place, finds it, and is able to save lives, there is nothing indifferent about such knowledge (even though the water dries up over time, the community moves, and this information ceases to be relevant). The person who is joyfully reunited with a loved one feared disappeared, the knowledge of the love between them is not the slightest bit illusory (even though that love may die down and resentment may build to the point of forcing a separation and even mutual hatred). For a family who has lost their house, jobs, tranquillity, and esteem because of new economic policies, there is nothing "false" in defining such policies as wrong (even though the majority of people see things very differently). Finally, for an indigenous community that has successfully overcome a certain sickness, there is nothing "deceptive" in that knowledge they share about the curative virtues of certain local natural medicines (even when official medical texts say that knowledge is superstitious).

Relative knowledge, whether true or false, does not necessarily mean that it is all the same. Some knowledge is vital, crucial, and urgent even when it is fleeting, incomplete, self-interested, and conjectural. Other knowledge, despite how permanent, detailed, disinterested, and fundamental it is, might leave the majority of the general population apathetic because it is not connected to the most pressing necessities and interests of the community.

Knowledge of What (Still) Isn't

We are used to regarding knowledge as real, as what exists or truly existed. At first glance, it seems absurd to speak about knowledge of something that never existed. Nonetheless, many forms of human knowledge, including all the sciences, frequently deal with what never existed.

We often hear that the prestige of modern science is due to its powers of prediction and its contribution to the development of extremely useful inventions. But what about the predictions in physics, chemistry, meteorology, astronomy, and geology? In general, what are predictions? They are affirmations that what hasn't existed will exist in the future, at least under certain conditions. Obviously, scientists don't always prove their predictions. They revise many theories while others fall apart. They repeat or criticize other experiments but rather than become dismayed, apparent setbacks stimulate them to continue their investigations.

And what are inventions but theoretical or material artifacts that never existed before but were known in the creative imaginations of their inventors?

When we maintain that things can be other than they appear or when we take the trouble to educate our children in differently—when we construct a new theory, take the necessary precautions before a flood, or invent a new solution to an old problem—we are affirming and exercising the human capacity of knowing what has never been and is not now.

There are communities dealing with exhausting and devastating problems every single day that mainstream knowledge will not solve. In such circumstances, it is all the more important and urgent to develop the capacity of knowing what hasn't existed before and of imagining what might be feasible, not only useful and desirable. This capacity nurtures the ideals and utopian ideas that make change, discovery, and invention possible.

Unfortunately, the dogmatic affirmation of certain utopias has also given rise to politics of terror and extermination. Examples abound, including the exploitation of Africa and the Americas by European dynasties; Stalin, Hitler, and Pol Pot; US policy in Vietnam and Iraq; and the World Bank and International Monetary Fund in the developing world. At the same time, what these utopias have most feared is awareness of the unknown: the shared dream of a new dawn after their living nightmares.

What "isn't" and what "doesn't exist" is not a simple matter. It encompasses what was and what will never be again, the forgotten and what we refuse to see, what is feared, despised, and longed for, what we do not believe is possible and what seems on the verge of happening, what we strive to give birth to and what we suspect will require enormous effort. Knowledge is also constructed of these very same materials, not only from direct experience with what already exists.

This has a lot to do with an interesting religious tradition in certain strains of Judaism, Christianity, and Buddhism. It is usually called negative theology. According to this tendency, we cannot know what God is, only what God is not. Knowledge of transcendence and the divine may derive from denials, exclusions, and disassociations but never from affirmation. This belief stems from a profoundly humble attitude about the sacred in our world and in the cosmos. It asserts that the reality of Spirit is much richer, deeper, varied, and dynamic than humans can understand and express in words. Aside from the contemplative silence of the mystic and the metaphor of the artist, negative theological knowledge gives us a way of imagining what God is not.

I would like to close this point by underscoring that the vast majority of contemporary mathematicians understand math not as an exact and definitive science but as a work of human genius and creativity. This human quality allows us to imagine what is not and to propose it so that it somehow becomes real.

Knowledge as Prejudging, Re-cognizing, and Co-knowing

Most of what we know doesn't come from direct experience but from distant experience that is somehow conveyed or communicated to us.

When Herman went to study in exile in Paris, it seemed to him that French workers were extremely rude and unpleasant. Every time he went into a store or office and stood before a noncommunicative functionary who seemed not to notice his arrival, Herman politely greeted him in his best French. Systematically, these clerks treated him in a brusque and rude manner. When he commented on this to Marlene, another exile who had been in Paris longer than he, she told him: "The same thing happened to me at first. One day, in a long line at the post office, I watched how other customers and clerks interacted and I realized that when the customer greets the worker first, the clerk feels interrupted, pressured, and underappreciated. The clerk views him as impolite and bad mannered, even if he speaks softly and is cheerful, and he counterattacks in order to defend himself and affirm his dignity. The trick is waiting for the clerk to say the first hello." Herman tried this out and marveled at the results! In everyday life, we function according to a series of prejudgments or prior opinions, many of which have been inherited from our surroundings, preceding generations, or the media. We perceive and judge the unknown on the basis of what is already known by us or others. Sometimes we fall into the trap of classifying what's truly new and different as good or bad, not merely unusual.

Human knowledge is not constructed in a vacuum. It does not start at zero. From the moment we first experience the world around us, probably in the womb, we receive a prefabricated and preconstructed world and an image of the world. We perceive everything from that vantage point. That's why knowing always consists of memory, remembrance, and recognition. If something seems familiar, we will re-cognize it, imagine and classify it as such, and behave accordingly. If experiencing something takes a toll on us, it's possible that we associate it with something strange that we lived through before, and we respond accordingly. But it can also stimulate our curiosity and inventiveness, giving birth to a new way of seeing reality.

Knowing, this prejudging and re-cognizing, is not just an individual task. It is always a collective, communal effort, and the wisdom imparted is derived from the common effort of many generations and peoples. Within a given world, we inherit an outlook, a mentality, and a language. Even when our knowledge is directed against that world, its mentality and languages continue being primary material and serve as points of constant reference and departure from everything we come to know.

We also acquire knowledge in dialogue with our peers. The problems we pose and the concepts with which we express them, how we resolve and communicate about them, and the answers we are hoping for—all this is part of the world that others created and we inherited. Thanks to the previous work carried out by a host of people, knowledge is possible. Because of it, we are able to keep a conversation going that can be public, conscientious, and careful. But it can also take the form of an unconscious interior monologue, observing certain rules of the game (the fruit of generations) that surpass pure individuality. To know, then, is to reknow—to try in concert with others to understand what interests us about our shared reality.

Knowledge as Misrecognition and Exaggeration

Some years ago, a friend with whom I had spoken about the need to be level headed and calm when investigating our reality posed this scenario for consideration: We are in a theater with hundreds of other people watching a controversial film. Suddenly, someone sees what they think is a time bomb under the seat of a spectator who just got up. "What do you do?" she asked. Calmly examine the object, with a level head, before saying anything? Return to watching the film and await a more appropriate moment to concern yourself with the suspicious object? Take an objective, cold, and rational step back, reasoning that it is only one object among millions and does not require any special attention? Place the value of your own life "in parentheses" and recognize that objective knowledge doesn't have anything to do with human actions and decisions? Of course not! Who in their right mind wouldn't try to get the crowd to exit the theater before the thing explodes and kills everyone! Whoever, in the name of objectivity and level-headedness, would favor that everyone remain seated and calmly analyze the predicament from every possible angle, we'd send them to the insane asylum while we run for our lives!

Often it is only possible to know a reality if we highlight and exaggerate one small aspect of it. Moreover, when a person or community faces crucial and urgent situations, knowing requires concentration and haste and an almost exclusive concern for what appears most serious and decisive. In such cases a level-headed, tolerant, and calm attitude can mean suicide, as was the tragic fate of many indigenous communities in America and Africa, the Jews in Europe during the Third Reich, democratic socialists in Hungary in 1956, residents of San Miguelito in Panama City during the US invasion in 1989, and countless others throughout history.

This also happens when we run up against something new and important, or with something familiar that has suddenly acquired a decisive magnitude. Then we tend to ignore it. To get people's attention and inspire them to participate in finding out what's new and take action, it's necessary to exaggerate, emphasize, and shout to the four winds what, because it's old or absurd, seems invisible.

Knowing is also unknowing, ignoring, or overlooking a good part of reality. Exaggeration and alarm can serve as a distraction. When we construct a new theory, we discount an infinite number of other possible theories. When we investigate something, we stop paying attention to thousands of other things and relationships right before our eyes. Giving importance to one dimension of reality, whether we want to or not, takes attention from something else and denies other dimensions. To concentrate on one aspect of reality, we act as though the rest of reality does not exist.

This is apparently how knowledge works, and it brings advantages, risks, and aspects of minimal importance, depending on the circumstances. Although it generally happens in an automatic, spontaneous, and unconscious way, this process of elimination or selection can also be systematic and deliberate.

If we dig in our heels and insist on seeing the big picture from every possible angle, not only won't we see anything, but we'll drive ourselves crazy or become paralyzed and unable to do anything. To perceive something and take action, active ignorance is necessary, at least temporarily.

In contrast, the need to reduce reality in order to see something can blind us to other equally or more important facts. Recognizing that what we do not know is infinitely greater that what we know can help us to be less arrogant, dogmatic, intolerant, and close minded. It can stimulate our curiosity or lead us to inaction and cynicism. It depends on things that go far beyond the theme of this book, such as our childhoods, values, feelings, and the seriousness of our actual needs.

Knowledge as Continuous Transformation

For reasons I do not understand very well, Westerners often share a prejudice that can make reading these reflections difficult. It is an attitude that regards only that which is universal, eternal, static, and perfect as good, true, just, and beautiful. But life is in a constant state of change, mutation, and it is situated somewhere in the cycle of life and death. Perhaps that's why we have invented this other prejudice, that of progress and development, which asserts that only that which advances toward a perfect, unchangeable, and eternal universality is good and true. Neither crises, ambiguity, and heterogeneity fit into this myth, causing many Westerners to associate progress with a cynicism, naked egoism, and pessimism (even optimism, for that matter), affirming that we are entering into the final and perfect phase of history.

Why will it take so much out of so many of us to regard beauty, truth, abundance, and justice as numerous, varied, changing, and relative—alive like life itself? This brings me to the subject of knowledge. I would like to propose that we see knowledge as multiple, heterogeneous, dynamic, and a vital part of life itself.

In particular, I want to reiterate that human knowledge is in constant transformation. I am not saying that knowledge should change. Instead I am acknowledging that in different societies, activities, disciplines, and theories, human awareness is incessantly changing and full of powerful dynamics, variety, conflicts, and novelties. I do not maintain that all this change represents progress. It's simply change, and not necessarily for the better or for worse.

In some societies and eras, there has been a search to know more deeply and achieve greater control of the surrounding reality. When this happens we can say that there was, in fact, a certain evolution, a progress and accumulation of awareness. It sometimes occurs in conjunction with bigger or smaller societies. It may last for varying lengths of time and experience a mutual heightening of awareness. But this is fairly rare and affects a small percentage of humanity.

I believe it is important to underscore that progress, whether it's scientific and technological advances or knowledge itself, is always confined to some generations and societies, and it encompasses only a handful of dimensions at any given time. It is important to be mindful of this, for it can help us maintain a humble and respectfully open attitude toward the possibly negative aspects of progress. After all, it is always possible that what represents progress in one place can mean a step back or stagnation somewhere else. And what brings progress to one community in the short term can cause harm in another, and even harm to both communities in the long run.

You could say that all of humanity shares a constant desire for improvement and advancement. This might indicate that humanity tends toward progress in spheres of knowledge and technology alike. Unfortunately, the only "universal progress" that we know at this point has been defined and imposed on subjugated peoples by empires all across the globe. Destruction and genocide have usually preceded and accompanied the very same progress to the point that we can say that setbacks have been even more common than progress.

Furthermore, phases of evolutionary change, progress, and accumulation of new knowledge frequently coincide with periods full of great disputes, new theories, and a radical departure from the accepted way of looking at things.

European experts in the health sciences from the nineteenth century viewed traditional peasant and indigenous medicine as primitive hocus-pocus. Experts today in the North Atlantic see their predecessors as little more than crude butchers. Thanks to psychoanalysis, feminism, ecology, democracy, information, migration, and an openness toward herbal medicine, many of us today critically evaluate the destructiveness and dogmatism of modern medicine.

These recent developments show that scientific and technological development are not just linear and universal, and there is no global progress and growth of human knowledge. Things are richer, much more complex and ambiguous, than the myth of scientific progress suggests. I am not proposing a negative, pessimistic, or cynical attitude regarding the hope for moral, technical, and cognitive progress. On the contrary, I am arguing that an open, humble, and self-critical attitude can inspire curiosity, creativity, research, and correction of our mistakes. An awareness of the limitations, ambiguities, and risks of all progress can serve us, much more than blind faith in technical and scientific progress, to foresee, evaluate, and correct much of the destructive potential of the development of knowledge and technology.

In this sense, I am not a supporter of a "unification" of human knowledge. I have greater appreciation for an openness to a numerous forms of knowledge, not simply complementary forms but mutually challenging, questioning, transforming, and enriching ones. The respectful dialogue that allows many ways of conceiving the world, life, and what constitutes progress can be more hopeful than submission to one sole way of seeing things. But would this signify true progress for all of humanity? I hope so! It depends on each and every one of us. And perhaps it demands verifiable worldwide disarmament beforehand, as there is very little chance of dialogue when one or some parties have the weapons with which they can impose their perspective and/or exterminate other actors on the world stage.

After all, if reality is in a state of continual metamorphosis, if different points of view proliferate and stimulate constant debate, if every answer offered to address an ancient problem provokes several new questions, if we ourselves, the people who live and love life and ask ourselves about it are constantly changing, how could we expect our knowing to be any different?

Another Way of Looking at the Question of Truth and Error
A friend from the United States told me about a woman who parachuted out of the plane over a forest that was completely foreign to her. She landed in a tree and got so hung up that it was impossible for her to touch the ground. After several hours in that condition, an elegantly dressed man walked beneath her just a few feet away. Desperately, she shouted,

"Hey, mister. Please help me! Look, up here! Tell me where I am!" Rather surprised, the man looked up and responded, "Well, you're hung up in a tree." The woman asked, "Are you a theologian?" He answered, "Yes, miss, I am. How did you know?" "By your answer, sir. It was absolutely true but completely useless!"

Without a doubt, this anecdote can be said about many professions. For example, there are those who say that there are two kinds of lies, true ones and statistics.

What I want to suggest is that this question of the truth (and the lie) is not so simple. On the one hand, Western intellectual tradition, which is dualistic and authoritarian, has taught us to regard the truth as radically incompatible with error, without any middle ground between the two. Furthermore, that tradition has trained us to conceive of truth as something principally intellectual, mental and cerebral, and that truth reflects reality and expresses it in words. Curiously, the truth is not affected by mental processes, changes in reality, or cultural and linguistic variety. According to this perspective, the truth would be the same the whole world around, regardless of time, place, age, sex, race, culture, language, religion, physical, emotional, and economic condition. It would be fixed, eternal, and independent of nearly everything else. Such a conception of truth seems characteristic of empires that are interested in (and capable of) subjecting other societies to their way of living and thinking, or in other words, to their truth.

Meanwhile, the experience of the past two centuries makes it more difficult to assert that reality is fixed and absolute. The information about living and past cultures; the great mutations and varied criticisms of nearly every great school of thought; the proliferation of conflicting and competing disciplines, theories, and beliefs; the rebellion of oppressed peoples and sectors who reclaim their rights and demand respect for their way of living, thinking, speaking, and dying—all this makes it extremely difficult to reduce the problem of the truth to simple formulas.

Perhaps we are lacking self-critical humility and expansive thinking. Why think about singular, abstract, and solitary truth, and not of the many truths that make sense in the everyday lives of varied communities and peoples? Why don't we conceive of truth as linked to the search for the good shared life, as emerging from practical and emotional demands and not only from the intellect? Can't we imagine these truths as radically necessary efforts that every human community experiences in a tangible way to articulate and communicate their perception of reality? Couldn't we understand that these efforts are not indifferent or illusory? They are absolutely serious, urgent, and decisive in the life of any community. Yet they are not universal, eternal, or fixed!

If we reexamine the problem of truth that way, couldn't we admit that the truths are profoundly important, particular, variable, and perishable—much like our own lives, families, institutions, and our maps? Couldn't we introduce an infinite range of intermediate possibilities between right and wrong? Couldn't we concede that life is full of useless truths and fertile lies? Wouldn't we become more capable of seeing the truths as insular links that have meaning and sense in specific communities? Couldn't we imagine that there are infinite truths and infinite ways of thinking and expressing each one?

Just as many indigenous communities, Eastern religions, and some branches of modern and ancient Judaism have done, couldn't we, too, arrive at a humble respect for truths that differ from ours and the right to proclaim ours in a thousand different ways? Wouldn't we eventually see these varied truths as equally human (or perhaps equally divine) and profoundly different, not better or worse? Couldn't we assume a humble, open, pluralistic, respectful, and solidarity perspective without being overwhelmed by the feeling that everything has lost its value and its meaning? Couldn't we appreciate even more deeply the value and the meaning of cultures, traditions, values, and knowledge—our own and others? Couldn't we even open ourselves up to reciprocal fertilization with communities that share truths that are different from ours? Wouldn't life be more bountiful? It's a shame that so many centuries of armed intolerance by the colonial powers has made it so difficult for the powerful and so dangerous for the oppressed to enter into a true, humble, and unarmed dialogue. Perhaps the only way of beginning to break this vicious cycle is to pursue a dialogue among those who are already disarmed. That means oppressed peoples and their communities.

Knowledge and Reality: Unity and Distinction

Omaira arrived in Mérida on a Friday afternoon to start her new job. On Saturday, she moved into a new apartment with friends. On Sunday she went to check out the shortest route between her house and the factory where she would be working. Great! It only took seven minutes from door to door on a day without much traffic. Wisely, she left home on Monday morning at 7:30, giving herself a half hour to drive to work. But all was in vain. She arrived at 8:02 (the traffic is always like this in the mornings, a coworker told her). Unhappy with that, Omaira tried a different route each morning. After three days she finally discovered a road on the outskirts of the city that was quiet, shady, and solitary, and though twice as long as the first road she took, it got her to work in less than twenty minutes. She later remarked that the shortest and easiest route isn't always the best.

A month later, at a work-related meeting at a penthouse in the center of the city, Omaira looked down on the street and spotted her original route. At the intersections, she saw that the drivers heading along the avenues blocked the cars trying to enter onto the main thoroughfares from the side streets. Of course, this clogged the traffic and slowed everything down. Omaira observed how strange it was, as everyone rushing to get to their destination as quickly as possible actually went much more slowly and arrived much later. She wondered aloud if things would change if everyone could see the situation as she did from the balcony.

That experience and Omaira's reflections seem useful for introducing the theme concerned with the relationship between knowledge and reality. Let me suggest that we think about knowledge and reality neither as separate nor as one and the same.

The image, or map, of reality that we make to guide us is influenced by our experience of that same reality. The shocks and jolts along the way sometimes force us to include, project, minimize, or discard aspects of map itself. But many of the conflicts result from our subjectivity, values, and prejudices. We always construct reality in relation to what affects, interests, attracts, or intimidates us. Said another way, the reality we know is, in a certain sense, "objectivity" that exists independently of us. But I would suggest that we know reality only when it affects and interests us, when, in essence, it forms part of our "subjectivity." Although I remain convinced that the best road between two points is the shortest one, many other possible routes will continue to exist without me.

That's the first idea regarding the differentiation and the link between knowledge and reality. The only reality that exists for us is that which we are interested in knowing about because it affects us in some way. What does not affect us does not exist until we are touched by it!

Grasping reality in one way, not another, causes us to behave in certain ways and not others. And our behavior is real. It's part of reality and modifies it. Although I remain convinced that the best way to get to my destination is by hurrying and blocking anyone else's passage, I will continue contributing to a huge waste of time and energy, more pollution, more aggression, and more medical and economic problems in my city. Similarly, if I view nature as an external and inexhaustible source of raw materials to satisfy human needs, that sense of reality can contribute to the destruction of the ozone layer, the disappearance of many vegetable and animal species, floods, and the depletion of natural resources.

In that sense, I would like to propose a second idea for consideration: Knowing is not simply an intellectual exercise outside of reality. It is real action, part of reality, affected within reality and with real consequences that are transformed by reality. In other words, a reality that is known in one way is another face of the very same reality known differently by others.

Perhaps these ideas are more true today, especially with respect to how we live on the earth, than they were in past centuries.

A BASIC SYNTHESIS AND A REDEFINITION

We have touched lightly upon several weighty aspects of the general problem of knowledge. We have talked about the sciences, truth, reason, the role of emotions, different aspects of the relativity of knowledge, and a facet of the relation between knowledge and reality. We have taken note of some criticisms of certain mainstream notions on these themes, and we have suggested possible avenues for alternative reflection and consideration. I hope that this is at least sufficient to spark surprise, curiosity, meditation, critical reflection, and open discussion by those who read these pages.

Now I would like to close this fifth and final chapter by proposing a redefinition of knowledge in light of all that we have looked at and suggested. I don't know if it will be worth anything, for the "last word" surely belongs to those who read, think about, and discuss the contents of this book. (I'd like to point out that there's no such thing as a last word as long as the human race still exists!)

First of all, I would propose conceiving of knowledge as the mental reconstruction of real relationships. Reconstruction: knowing is the task carried out within a vision of reality that is inherited from and shared by at least some of our peers (prefabricated reality is the point of departure, the raw material and the environment within which we recognize reality). Reconstruction: knowing is not just copying reality, nor is it *adaequation rei et intellectual*, that is, that the intellect of the knower must be adequate to the known, the thing or separate reality that is grasped. Reconstruction of reality: knowledge is not the simple reproduction of reality but the active selection and creative reorganization of elements of real experience and the production of images, visions, concepts, or maps of reality. Mental reconstruction: knowledge as a reconstruction of what is real is worked out in the soul and our personal and shared subjectivity. Mental reconstruction of real relationships: because it's not isolated objects or things that we reconstruct in order to know; what we mentally reconstruct are links and networks of linkages of which we form a part (the objects would be like knots in a network where various relationships cross at once). Mental reconstruction of real relationships: it's not a matter of abstract whimsy, except for running into relationships that touch, interest, and affect us, where we see ourselves forced to produce maps of reality or knowledge.

Beyond that, I would propose consideration of all knowledge as if it were a fragmentary, self-interested, imaginary, and fleeting reconstruction of reality. Fragmentary reconstruction: what we know are just pieces of reality stemming from our own experiences and the experiences of our peers (and what we don't know may be infinitely greater than what we can come to know or imagine, collectively or alone).

Prejudiced or biased reconstruction: what we know we always grasp from an ensemble of interests, prejudices, values, loyalties, emotions, feelings, bonds, apprehensions, traditions, habits, dreams, and projects. These orient and limit our attention like the choice of perspective, spokespeople, themes, methods, and resources. Without a doubt, we can critically reflect on the interested gaze, but we are never totally outside of it.

Imaginary, creative, and presumptuous reconstruction: we try not to see knowledge as a copy or reflection of anything. Knowing can be conceived, among other things, as the serious human effort of actively and creatively imagining certain relationships, structures, and processes in reality. (I would even dare to say that it is an artistic process.) We can look at knowledge as a constant hypothetical exercise in making maps, metaphors, and other skills in order to understand how to articulate and affect the reality surrounding us.

Finally, transitory, provisional reconstruction: despite the fact that there are some cultures in which the maternal lineage of the vision of the world has remained the same for thousands of years, there is no knowledge that is safe, intact, and accepted by all members of the human family. Constant transformations of reality, the multiplication of perspectives, internal conflicts in human societies, the challenges and innovations that characterize all experience, the limitations of our cognitive capacity as well as our boundless creativity—all this, together with the inexhaustible richness of what's real, suggests the transitory nature of all knowledge, science, and truth. It is always easy to differentiate "the same" from another way that has been elaborated up to a certain moment partly because "the same" never really is the same or equal. I am aware that this way of conceiving knowledge is barely an entrée to the endless ideas from the past, the present, and the future. I am not sure that this way of seeing things, or even my values and interests, are the best. However, I am convinced that in times of crisis and pessimism like today in the Americas, whoever doesn't run the risk of making a mistake has already lost. I prefer the Tibetan saying "When in doubt, act" to the Western "When in doubt, abstain."

I understand this way of conceiving knowledge as a provocative invitation to constantly confront our knowledge with the ever-changing reality; to respectfully and openly dialogue with every community and person that, disarmed and in a state of peace, would like to share different takes on reality; to release all of our inventiveness, creativity, and imagination and use these gifts and skills to ponder life in more constructive, peaceful, cooperative, and loving ways than the ones that dominate the world today; to daringly exercise our capacity for critical, communitarian, and personal reflection about the things that seem most obvious and evident.

I don't believe that this is about increasing or simply substituting at our knowledge, even less about arriving at a common and universal vision of reality. Possibly it concerns something very different: the opening, bending, criticizing, enriching, and incessant remaking of our knowledge of what is real in light of other communities with varied visions of reality. Perhaps. But I stress that it is difficult to honestly do this when our life is based on the pain of others. Imposing our knowledge on others is arrogant.

Nor is it easy at the other extreme when we are drained by the daily bustle of maintaining a family in the midst of severe shortages and insecurity. At the same time, a dialogue about knowledge is more urgent than ever but is feasible only against the wind and the waves.

Dialogue demands mutual vulnerability, trust, and tenderness. Perhaps only on the outside or under oppressive conditions is it possible to think about knowledge as a partial, presumptuous, and provisional reconstruction of our relationships. Because only then are we really interested in constructing life in a different way, in contrast to how it seems in our day, condemned to premature death (am I perhaps too pessimistic?).

❧ Conclusions

While rereading and revising the last chapter, I feel that, to a certain point, these meditations on knowledge that I wish to share with you are already there—and there is very little that I would add for now. However, it is an old custom of mine to suggest to my students that they always end every essay with some conclusions, reflections that will summarize what has been expressed, thus opening a door to invite the readers to continue beyond the text in a certain direction.

I am going to opt here for a combination of these approaches. First, I am going to share—differently than in the introduction—some aspects of the process from which these meditations emerged. Later, in closing, let me invite you to reflect upon the importance of the questions—more than the importance of the certainties—that we bear throughout our lives.

FROM PAST CERTAINTIES TO THE UNCERTAIN SEARCH FOR THE FUTURE

In the Americas, we find ourselves in a situation that is painful, unprecedented, and, in many ways, disconcerting: we are drowning in the crisis of capitalism; the authoritarian socialist crisis has revealed that there was not much hope behind certain revolutionary flags: the timid socioeconomic experiments with democracy carried out by the Nicaraguan Sandinistas and Haiti's Lavalas movement seem to have suffocated under the intolerance of the powerful; the fresh wind of change that once blew among the young, the poor, and the churches, since the late 1960s, appears to have succumbed before the conservative onslaught. Even the feminist movement, with its encouraging growth within one generation, seems now to be suffering the battering of a great counterattack.

Many of the solid convictions that motivated many people to fight for the transformation of our society have been weakened or demolished in these transformations.

We "knew," in a sense, that somehow things would improve now that nearly all the countries of the Americas are politically democratic; we "knew" that, in general, the people would choose progressive leaders to guide our countries during this millennium. Or at least, that even if the elected were "others," we would somehow begin to come out of the nightmare in which the continent has been living. Unfortunately, the elected have been Fernando Henrique Cardoso, Carlos Menem, Bill Clinton, Alberto Fujimori, and Violeta Chamorro, who have, along with Carlos Andrés Pérez and others, presided over the increase in hunger, violence, unemployment, and corruption that overshadows our countries.[1] Meanwhile, grassroots organizations and movements—as well as the victories that these have achieved in the past—lose ground year after year. Many of us also "knew" that socialism was better than capitalism, and that as a result, it would win in any confrontation. Now we no longer know. It has been not only the overthrow of true socialism that contradicts our "knowing" but also the massive popular opposition to socialism in the very places where it was practiced and the discovery of crimes that we believed could occur only under capitalism (including ecological and medical crimes, as well as massive administrative corruption).

We "knew" that the churches, particularly the traditional ones, would continue exploring the option of liberation of the oppressed that re-emerged in the 1960s, that the ecclesiastic community would grow in numbers and in influence, and that the liberation theologies would become a hopeful motivation for most pastors and church activists. Now we are seeing more and more churches applying predominantly authoritarian and conservative policies both internally and externally while base communities decrease in number, energy, and institutional support. The same liberation theologies seem to be incapable of providing a hopeful answer to the present crisis of capitalisms and socialisms, whereas churches that oppose ecumenical dialogue and are unconcerned about human rights seem to be popping up everywhere.

We "knew" that women's rights would become more and more recognized, that women would achieve greater respect and be more motivated in their creative, decision-making, and leadership skills. On the contrary, we are now faced with the fact that women constitute the majority among the poor, and they are poorer than men; that in many countries the laws that favor women are being or have been abolished; and that in the early years of the new century, from Alaska to Patagonia, all manner of violence against women has intensified.

We somehow now "know" that we really did not "know" and consequently, many of us feel lost, adrift, confused, and hopeless. Some of us fear having no reason left to continue fighting (there are even those who fear not having any reason left for living, having given so much of their lives in the struggle for a more humane hemisphere). Some others are attracted to the cry of "Run for your life!" and are inclined to devote themselves to only protect and enjoy, and if at all possible, to improve their own small, private individual or family life. Many of us experience a degree of resentment for the unrecoverable years of struggle (loved ones, relationships, family, home, work, studies, time, energy, and money), which, at times, now seem absurd.

A peculiar "crisis of knowledge" appears to be a part of the general crisis of our present societies. Within this crisis, some suspicions emerge that feed many of the reflections that I have mentioned in the previous pages. For example, we suspect that we have bestowed a naive, exaggerated trust in our capacity to simply know what is, just for what it is. We feel that this trust systematically leads us to not only deceive ourselves but also to authoritatively impose on others what we consider to be correct. We suspect that we have a strong inclination to see knowledge as being only one thing, and therefore to think that *other* forms of conceiving reality are necessarily wrong and should be eliminated "rationally" or through repression. We mistrust the conviction that knowledge of a reality somehow guarantees the success of achieving what one seeks at the heart of such a reality. We begin to recognize that the bonds between knowledge and practical success are very complex, varied, and as difficult to achieve as they are to control. We begin to speculate that the perception of reality through closed, dualist categories (e.g., true and false, good and bad, conservative and progressive) or even tripartite hypotheses (capitalism, socialism, and other options) encumbers rather than favors both the understanding of reality and a dialogue with people who may share different views on the matter.

Something similar happens with the naively optimistic view that sees human history developing in stages, in a continuous line that progresses inexorably from a lesser to a greater degree of knowledge, liberty, rationality, wealth, happiness, peace, justice, cooperation, and control of nature. We suspect, once again, that things are much richer, more heterogeneous, and more complex than suggested by the myths of progress, development, and evolution.

Finally, we question the credit and power we have attributed to the sciences, to scientific specialization, and to experts in a wide range of fields. We think that in doing so, we have tragically abdicated our capacity as well as our responsibility to participate in the construction, evaluation, and transformation of the knowledge of reality—and of the decisions based on such knowledge that affect our lives.

All this seems to indicate to us that the prevailing ways of knowing in our Western societies are more *a part of the problem* than of the solution to the present crisis. It seems as though these ways of knowing do not allow us either to truly understand or to extricate ourselves. Furthermore, even more clearly, we begin to perceive these ways of knowing as destructive, authoritarian, and antidemocratic; as stimulants to behavior, relationships, and institutions that are equally destructive, authoritarian, and antidemocratic. However, in general, now that we have begun to be aware of these things, we do not know what to do to extricate ourselves from this crisis of knowledge, from this uncertainty regarding which paths to take in the years to come. Sometimes, each one of us believes that this crisis is mainly one's own, personal, intimate matter. And since there are so many of us feeling the same way—hiding our perplexities and confusion—we do not dare take the first step toward sharing, with someone we trust, the search for ways to move beyond the confusion and paralysis.

But it just happens that there are many of us—probably millions—who today in the Americas share this restlessness. And it is good to know; it relieves the anguish and guilt of believing that this crisis of knowledge (of not truly knowing anymore what is going on, or why, or what to do to transcend it) is something purely individual. Besides, it provides the opportunity and the resources to together try to understand what is taking place and to discover paths—in theory and practice—to confront the present challenges in a new way.

These reflections have tried to be something of the latter: a way to share frustrations, doubts, searches, and intuitions of my own, yes, but ones that I have come to discover are also shared by millions of other people who dream of a better life for their children; a way, therefore, of relieving the anguish and personal guilt by sharing them with others who feel the same discomfort; a way, nevertheless, of finding company as we go along—offering reciprocal support, ideas, resources, and energy—to try to create escape routes for our hemisphere. I hope that this effort is of some value to other persons besides myself.

SHARED QUEST(ION)S RATHER THAN
PREFABRICATED ANSWERS

Perhaps one of the many bad habits of Westerners is to define, classify, and judge other people and cultures by the answers they provide to our questions. But what if our questions are not at all significant to these people? And besides, who can say that others understand our questions in the same way that we understand them? Isn't it possible that the "same" question can be understood and answered in many different ways? And finally, who can guarantee that the real consequences of answering a question in a certain way are the same for different people or communities?

Perhaps one really needs to question that bad Western habit of labeling, pigeonholing, and condemning others because of their answers to our questions. Perhaps—this is something of what I want to suggest in concluding these reflections—the important, the significant, and the decisive issues in life should not really be the answers we give to the questions of others but instead the *questions, concerns,* and *issues* that guide our lives and our ties to the rest of humanity and all creation. Perhaps one of the tragedies of Western cultures (the tragedy of Christianity, capitalism, and socialism, among other movements) is that, too frequently, we have clung to certain answers that we have found to our original questions, and in so doing, we have stopped the quest that served as a foundation for many our traditions.

Allow me to be somewhat ironic. Many questions are not "real." In other words, they are not questions that really seek to enrich personal knowledge or the life of a community; rather, they seek to find things to affirm or confirm the power of some people over others. They are, for example, the questions asked by someone who is arrogantly certain of possessing the correct answer and who is looking for one of two things: to ridicule the person being interrogated, thus "proving" how "wrong" he or she is, or to "control" the person being questioned, to see how much and what he or she knows, in order to classify the person according to some hierarchy and to give him or her instructions as to how to reach the top by stepping on the rest.

Besides, many of our questions are artificial; they are not really *ours*: they are merely the questions that are constantly thrown at us by the media or the power elite; they are merely the questions we have become accustomed to because it is more comfortable to do so, or we have done so out of fear; and they are, above all, the questions that do not cause us discomfort, because they already come with prefabricated and prepackaged answers. They are not questions that ask, revive, or nurture our lives or bonds with others. They are not true questions.

I would call *true questions* those concerns that we have considered deeply important and urgent in life but for which we do not believe we have answers (and perhaps no one ever had or will have a definite answer). They are the concerns that drive people to seek out the advice and answers of others, or to see if together they can construct provisional answers that could be helpful in such questions; or at least to see if by sharing the perplexity and personal anguish, one can find the necessary affection, understanding, and hope to continue to give thanks in prayer while living out one's life in an endless search for answers to the main concerns of life itself.

I believe that part of what we need today is precisely to listen attentively and humbly to the questions posed by "others"—people from other regions, cultures, and social classes—and reflect upon what their concerns can contribute to our own lives.

The Spanish poet Antonio Machado wrote, in his famous *Proverbios y cantares*, collected in his 1912 book *Campos de Castilla*:[2] "Wanderer, there is no road, the road is made by walking." The same could be applied to these answers: there are no answers; the answers come as you tread the path with the burden of certain questions. Perhaps what best defines the life of a common human being is not answers but the concerns he or she bears. The questions are what pressure one to search, create, think, imagine, invent, transform, improve, enrich, worry, attend to, care, engage in dialogue, listen, and give. The answers, in contrast—especially if taken too seriously, definitively, and conclusively, thus closing our ears to other attempts at answers and different concerns—run a greater risk of paralyzing, congealing, closing, and imposing. One could even say, "Tell me what you ask yourself, and I will tell you who you are."

Let us imagine someone who constantly asks him- or herself, for example, "What could I do to improve the lives of those around me? What negative consequences would my values, beliefs, and behavior have upon them?" Whoever lives with the burden of these questions—and even more so if they are deeply felt and lived, assuming the best answers as a kind of transitory imperative—will most likely do more good and less harm to people than those who live attached to unquestionable solutions.

This brings to mind the brief intellectual autobiography of the British philosopher and historian R. G. Collingwood, *The Idea of History*.[3] In this book, Collingwood maintains the interesting idea that all truth (and all error) is always truth (or error) in relation to a question. The same proposition can be true, false, indifferent, or impertinent, depending on the question that is to be answered in reference to the statement made. And consequently, there is no sense in examining the "truth" of a proposition, explanation or theory without first examining—and seriously considering—the questions that we are trying to answer.

Whoever reads this book will see that it does not intend to insinuate answers so much as to propose, communicate, multiply, and share *true* questions: concerns that I have been bearing for years for which I have no clear or definitive answers; enigmas for which I do not believe—and perhaps do not want to believe—that there can be only one conclusive answer; a continued search that will help keep me restless, alive, researching, listening, experimenting, imagining, evaluating, and transforming my own life; concerns that I prefer to bear instead of destroying them with answers.

I believe, hope, deeply wish, that the authentic questions of those who read this book, along with the ones included in these meditations, and those that may emerge as a result of joining them, will help in the development of theories of knowledge, sociopolitical guidance, truly *democratic* ethical reflections and theological essays: in other words, where community dialogue will lead to provisional consensus—always open to revision and transformation through the initiative of the community affected by such consensus—guided by the Spirit of Life, by the inner impulse to tenderly care for life, and above all for the lives of the most fragile and vulnerable (the children and the oppressed). So be it.

❧ Appendixes

ᴥ An(other) Invitation to Epistemological Humility: Notes toward a Self-Critical Approach to Counter-Knowledges

It is only when the dominated have the material and symbolic means of rejecting the definition of the real that is imposed on them . . . that the arbitrary principles of the prevailing classification can appear as such.
—PIERRE BOURDIEU, *Outline of a Theory of Practice*

In this essay, written as a series of short (hypo)theses, I try to construct an invitation to rethink our understandings of knowledge and truth from a perspective that I would call epistemological humility (as opposed to the epistemological arrogance of thinking that *we*—whoever *we* are—already have the definitive true knowledge of anything). This effort is explicitly and constantly inspired by the works of Pierre Bourdieu.[1] It is an effort animated by the idea that oppression, exclusion, domination, and exploitation often bring forth and stimulate the production of "counter-knowledges" (knowledges and ways of knowing opposed to the dominant ones), among many other consequences (most of them destructive), while paradoxically often contributing to, and (only partially) benefiting from, certain new forms of epistemological arrogance, which, somewhat as a result of producing knowledge from within a subaltern position, might often turn out to function as a self-defeating epistemology rather than the opposite. Connections with ethics and politics, and particularly with democracy, justice, and peace, are at the heart of this effort.

The predicament of Latino men and women in the United States—as agents of knowledge while objects of oppression, exclusion, domination, and exploitation—is what underlies and prompts this invitation. Placed, on the one hand, under the power of imperial policies toward Latin America, the greed of US national elites, the racism of its "white" (dwindling) majority, and, on the other hand, the often contradictory urgencies of survival, solidarity, adjustment, and/or success, Latinos in the United States are often urged (e.g., by past experience, personal qualms, traditional wisdom, nontraditional approaches) to question, doubt, and challenge what they are concurrently pressured, expected, and/or taught by the dominant culture to accept as true. Such a predicament can at times result in the production of counter-knowledges: alternative ideas, subversive discourses, dissident voices. However, one of the tragedies and tendencies of all knowledge produced within and under relations of oppression, exclusion, domination, and exploitation is that inadvertently, surreptitiously, at least part of the ruling patterns, relations, conceptions, and/or values permeating the larger society might be reintroduced. Thus, there is no guarantee that any counter-knowledge will forever and/or wholly avoid ending up reinforcing (rather than weakening) the prevailing ways of knowing against which it emerged (i.e., hierarchical, binary, authoritarian, patriarchal, racist, elitist ways of knowing). There is, however, always chance, hope, and room for a constant self-critique—individual and collective—of our counter-knowledges, alongside the possibility that such collective self-critique helps weaken, rather than buttress, the unavoidable tendency of subaltern counter-knowledges to wind up co-opted by and/or confirming the leading ways of knowing.

It is mainly to such constant self-critique of our counter-knowledges that I want to contribute the hypotheses here, especially as they might be useful for some Latina/o activists, leaders, and thinkers within the geographic, bodily, relational, institutional, mental, and spiritual territories currently occupied by the patriarchal, "white," neoliberal, capitalist, imperial global expansion headed by the United States.

(HYPO)THESES

I

Whatever we understand by knowledge, we always and only know in community, in a culture and a language shared by a community; a shared culture and language allow us to communicate what is understood, challenged, or probed as being—or not being—knowledge. In another culture or language we could easily be at a total loss, at least at first, to claim having, achieving, or conveying anything as knowledge.

This is markedly important for Latin American immigrants, their US Latino descendants, and their relatives gradually turned into *aliens*—by xenophobia, racism, and/or the ever-moving western and southern frontiers ("we didn't cross the border, the border crossed us" is a piece of grassroots counter-knowledge, among many others, shared by many Puerto Ricans and Mexican Americans).

Part of the social paradox of knowing is that knowledge is not yet quite knowledge unless and until it is recognized as such by a group of people—both in the sense of being "understood" by them and in the sense of being "accepted" by the group. If nobody understands or (what is almost the same, but not quite) if nobody accepts what somebody "knows," for all intents and purposes that knower knows nothing (for the time being); that is, that knower's knowledge (his, her, their knowledge) is at least provisionally incapable of making a difference in the community where the knower is located.

"Individual" knowledge is never merely individual: it is always a knowledge claimed by an individual within a community, but it is not quite yet knowledge until it is understood and validated by a community (or another). Or, otherwise stated, knowledge is always in process, in an unpredictable process for that matter, and knowledge is always in struggle: the process and the struggle of trying to (re)formulate (received or "new") knowledge in such a way as to gain understanding and acceptance (recognition), indeed, but also the process and the struggle of reacting and responding to the obstacles to such knowledge's being received and acknowledged as knowledge.

Even in the extreme, hypothetical case of a hermit separated from any human contact for decades, and suffering from what could be deemed (from the outside) as dementia, whatever the hermit knows cannot be so but in response to, and with the elements of, what he or she has acquired in the community in the years before being estranged from human contact—and it is on such a basis that the hermit's creativity might build. Whatever the hermit knows, it will not be understood and recognized as knowledge, again, unless and until a group of people concurs with it.

Changes, conflicts, and power dynamics in any community—unavoidable traits of any group of people, especially when time, size, innovations, and social differentiation intervene—have consequences in the ways in which knowledge is (differentially) understood and "used" within human interaction. For starters, those alterations, struggles, and forces at work tend to induce analogous changes, conflicts, and power struggles around what people want (or desperately need) to make sense of, to know, what we recognize (or overlook, or disqualify) as knowledge, and those whom we recognize (or dismiss) as producers or carriers of legitimate knowledge, as authorities.

II

Whatever we understand by knowing or knowledge (or, by extension, by true or truth), we almost invariably know amid unstable, asymmetric power relations, interests, and dynamics. The old dictum that knowledge is power probably contains more (and more problematic) wisdom than what we usually would want to grant it. To know is always, at least implicitly, a claim to know, and thus an attempt to either reaffirm "what everybody knows" (and thus gain recognition as a normal, acceptable member of the community) or to sway others toward a more or less novel way of understanding (and thus gain recognition as a legitimate challenger of accepted verities). Claiming to know something, to have knowledge, is thus always a kind of claim to power, a political move.

Knowledge might simply be, to begin with, a claim to share and accept what all or most (or those with the weightiest say) in a community accept and share as true, obvious, mandatory, expected, or the like (as in "we all know that *undocumented*, *illegal*, and *criminal* go together"). That is, it might be a way of claiming that the present, prevailing state of affairs is OK, is as it should be, and needs not be challenged. Therefore, (claiming) knowledge might entail a surreptitious threat to whoever dares to even think of challenging the prevailing power arrangements in the community (be such community a family, a network of specialized scientific experts, a nation, a political constituency, a hospital, a religious congregation): a subtle summons to acquiesce to the establishment.

Knowing, however, may involve a claim to know something that others do not know: a claim to a "new" or "hidden" knowledge, one that does not fully mesh either with the prevailing power arrangements in the community or with the established epistemological order therein (i.e., the limits of what is socially accepted to be known and knowable). Think of the claim, "First-generation immigrants have a significantly lower rate of involvement in criminal activities than US-born, third-generation or higher, 'white' citizens."

An utterance is then, more often than not (and regardless of the awareness of the "speaker"), simultaneously an epistemological and a political act(ion): awakening, activating, mobilizing not only knowledge(s) (within a wide range of possibilities going from confirmation of the prevailing state of affairs to its questioning, interruption, and/or subversion), including in the "speaker" her- or himself as well as in her or his web of relations—but also awakening, activating, mobilizing power claims, relations, struggles, conflicts, fears, and other types of conflictual dynamics.

In fact, most utterances could be seen as being in themselves, at least to a certain degree, claims to power, to authority: appeals to assent, respect, and recognition—that is, political moves. This is particularly the case when and/or if such an utterance commands (or tries to bring forth) attention—an attempt that is more likely to succeed if and/or when the person uttering something is capable of mobilizing significant forces (e.g., social, economic, military, political, legal, emotional) behind her or his utterances, or at least of giving the appearance and stirring the fear of having such capability.

Conversely, the "same" utterance (as seen abstractly by an "outsider"), even in the "same" community, but uttered by a different or differently located "speaker" (or by the "same" one but in a different juncture in the dynamics of the "same" community) might be entirely "inaudible," overlooked, meaningless—or worse: it might elicit rejoinders, attacks, violent silencing, or even physical suppression.

Or, to put it in yet other terms: no utterance (written, sung, spoken, iconic, gestured, or otherwise) can have only one meaning in or of itself, because meaning is not something residing in the utterance, or even in the utterer, but, rather, it is produced and can be "present" only in the relation (itself unstable and perishable) between utterance (and, if somehow present, its utterer, too) and a community of interpretation—the latter equally unstable, mobile, perishable.

Meaning is located always in an unstable relation—a relation, among other things, of course, of knowledge, inexorably located amid a dynamic, larger constellation of relations, which indeed complicate the production, circulation, perception, and transformation of meaning (i.e., of knowledge): relations of identity, competition, exchange, power, domination, resistance, alliance, and so on, which include (but are by no means limited to) gender, sexual, economic, political, cultural, linguistic, military, and other types of relations, many of which (but not necessarily all, nor all necessarily reinforcing each other) involve lopsided, asymmetric, conflictual power dynamics.

Thus, the meaning of an utterance, if any, is (re)produced in relation (both specific and variable) to the history, culture, and dynamics (including power dynamics) of a specific community—be these personified in one single individual member of a community having access to that utterance or embodied in a group.

This suggests that, in all probability, any utterance can mean anything—including what would seem from certain perspectives as absolute opposite meanings—depending on the interest and/or knack of the "hearer(s)" (e.g., reader, dancer, singer, preacher, professor) to (re)produce a particular meaning, as well as on her, his, or their ability to mobilize certain forces (e.g., social, political, legal, emotional) both in favor of such meaning and over against those different or opposite understandings of the "same" utterance (and against the bearers of those other differing senses).

What is needed to transform a certain, accepted meaning, of a "stable" discourse (e.g., text, icon, song) in a particular community into what would have been typically grasped in that same community as its exact opposite meaning is at least, probably, time (which helps forget and transform meanings), people (i.e., increased numbers of individuals and groups invested in the "new" meaning), and power (of any and/or all sorts) to both boost the "new" meaning and to counter the lingering or reemerging remembrance, allegiances, and diffusion of former meanings of the "same" discourse or utterance. Is this not what happens in many of our churches with the ancient Hebrew injunction regarding hospitality to the stranger?

III

Whatever we understand by knowing or knowledge, we could submit that it is less so (held less and by fewer people as knowledge, as "real," as "true"), the less the attention, importance, and consequences (as well as denials, refutations, rejections, and dismissals) it is capable of bringing forth—and it is more of a knowledge (held more and by more people in a community as knowledge, as "real," as "true"), the more interest, significance, and effects (no less than its denials, refutations, rejections, and dismissals) it is able to elicit. In other words, knowledge is something that (like love?) has a thinner, weaker "reality," the weaker, thinner, and more fragile the bonds among those "sharing" it are—it basically dissolves if and/or as the interest in it (and/or the community sharing such interest) fades away, disintegrates, or dies out.

Knowledge and the interest that constitutes it as such, the importance giving it weight in a community, the recognition it awakens, and the authority it carries (or not), all require previous and concomitant labor, an "intellectual" labor of thinking, rethinking, presenting, arguing, refuting, persuading, and so on. In addition, emotional, physical, erotic, political, economic, linguistic, aesthetic, legal, cultural, police, military, and other types of labor might be necessary and/or helpful to generate, sustain, disseminate, defend, enforce, and reinforce what appears to the community as the most "important" knowledge(s), chiefly if and/or when other competing interests (and related knowledge or knowledges and groups) threaten the consensus supporting the prevailing knowledge(s)—and therefore the power of the groups and relations linked to it.

Whatever is shared, recognized, and accepted in a certain community as knowledge (i.e., not merely as perception or opinion, but as an important, authoritative, "true" knowledge) is such as a result of the investment of time and energy in constructing and safeguarding such knowledge as valid, legitimate, true, and important. In this sense, knowledge is accumulated labor.

Diplomas, awards, publications, reviews, interviews, citations, invitations, appointments, salaries, promotions, and so on—as Pierre Bourdieu, among others, has tirelessly endeavored to understand, analyze, and demonstrate—are often distinctions recognizing such accumulated, embodied labor (i.e., the number of hours, dollars, and connections collectively invested in being admitted, trained, promoted, and recognized as a holder of and an authority in a certain type of knowledge).

In this sense, knowledge is capital—one peculiar form of capital, which, as all forms of capital, might be used to acquire other forms of capital and might serve to enhance, reinforce, and protect different forms of capital "owned" by the "knower," those associated with her or him, as well as the institutions of which she or he is part.

To acquire the only form of knowledge that is worth anything in a particular community, that is, recognized knowledge or knowledge acknowledged and respected as such (as distinction, as capital, as worth, as value), a certain type of labor is required that calls for a certain degree or amount of time, energy, self-esteem, acknowledgment, training, and so on. Most people in most modern societies have not enough of these resources readily available to them so as to acquire and/or produce enough recognized knowledge to elicit the attention, respect, and recognition beyond, at the very best, a certain modicum of deference among a reduced group of acquaintances.

As with other forms of capital (in modern societies at least), the more widely known something is, and known by a larger diversity of people, the less important it is. Otherwise stated, the more common, easily attainable, and widespread a certain type of knowledge becomes, the less valued, appreciated, esteemed, distinctive, and respected it becomes. The less often it is recognized as important, interesting knowledge, the less it will command attention, prestige, action, or obedience.

No wonder, first, that so many people, doubting their own capacity to know, for having been subject to decades of humiliation, invisibility, neglect, marginalization, abuse, and/or exploitation—without ever enjoying the respect and attention (i.e., the love) that could have awakened and nurtured in them at least the energy, self-esteem, and recognition necessary to produce recognized knowledge—end up seeking knowledge, meaning, and truth outside of themselves and their kin, among those already esteemed and recognized by most as authorities, experts, people who really know and who know what is really important. Think of a Hispanic child uttering (or not quite yet: deciding whether to utter) her dissenting knowledge of the pronunciation, use, or meaning of a Spanish word in a classroom where she frequently finds herself bullied by her classmates and/or scorned by the teacher, when not simply invisible, unheard, nonexistent.

No wonder, symmetrically, that, for their part, those already esteemed and recognized by most as intellectual authorities, as experts, as the people who really know, and who know what is really important, try (without knowing that they are trying) to keep their knowledge rare, either by "giving" of it only that modicum that they deem accessible to the populace (somehow letting the recipients know that this is the case and earning recognition for their charitable donations) or by denying that knowledge to the common folk, clothing their wisdom in esoteric, obscure, "specialized" jargon, thus redoubling their distinctive preeminence as experts with an impossibility of being understood save by their peers.

Unless acutely aware of such complementary epistemological tendencies between elites and the subaltern, the very groups and individuals engaged in an intellectual struggle (supposedly) in solidarity with the oppressed and against the dominant elites, might easily end up swallowed by those same dynamics of intellectual distinction, carving secondary niches of expertise (e.g., in churches, unions, nongovernmental organizations, opposition parties), where authority, recognition, connections, self-esteem, and other forms of capital can be accumulated and later exchanged for yet further types of capital—probably contributing, in the end, not to dismantle but to reinforce and further veil the role of (recognized) knowledge (theirs included) in the reproduction and cover-up of relations of domination. Ironically, this is at times the case with Bourdieu's thought and jargon—originally supposed to have emerged to expose elitist relations and oppressive hierarchies, but every so often used instead to re-create and reinforce dynamics of exclusion and self-aggrandizement.

Nobody is exempt from the temptation and possibility of slowly sliding from (honestly believing that they are) producing and using their knowledge mainly in the service of vulnerable, at-risk populations, to using the privileged position of the "intellectual" among the subaltern (and to increasingly orient their production of knowledge) to secure, enhance, and reinforce their own position of privilege—thus enabling themselves to accumulate enough capital (e.g., relations, prestige, self-esteem) to exchange for positions in other social locations, including in the service of the dominant power structures and elites. I submit that, rather than an anomaly, this is the "normal" (tragic) tendency of intellectuals, especially when we refuse to acknowledge that this is the normal tendency and to take the necessary collective measures to counter it.

IV

The easy opposition between knowledge, on the one hand, and illusion, falsehood, ignorance, and the like, on the other—an opposition that is but the inverse of the almost natural, spontaneous identification of knowledge with "truth," "reality," and "the facts"—deserves to be critically analyzed as both an outcome and an instrument of the long labor of imposition of certain forms of knowledge (certain "knowledges") over and against competing claims and interests; this imposition being, more often than not, one more strategy (not necessarily conscious or deliberate, and all the more efficient if it is *not* conscious or deliberate) in the complex struggle of the dominant elites to at least preserve the power (of any and all types) thus far accumulated, to ward off threats to such accumulated power and, if feasible, to reinforce and broaden that power.

Intellectuals, including composers, poets, theologians, storytellers, teachers, reporters, editors, novelists, philosophers, historians, economists, preachers, ministers, union leaders, and so on (i.e., people who produce and distribute one or another type of "knowledge"), all too often tend to identify my and/or our knowledge as "the" truth, reality, and the facts—and to cast the differing, competing knowledges as erroneous, false, wrong, or, at worst, as deliberate deceit.

The easy opposition between "truth" (i.e., the knowledge we agree with) and "error" (the knowledge that we disagree with and that therefore we refuse to recognize as knowledge) might be, especially for subaltern, dominated, marginalized groups, both necessary in the short run and self-destructive in the middle and long runs. Or, otherwise stated, the opposition might be in the end exclusively beneficial to those who have already attained enough power in a society so as to monopolize the epistemological power of defining which knowledge is knowledge, true and worthwhile, and which is not, thus doomed to ridicule, oblivion, justifiable suppression, or, at best, to be the relic of a surmounted past.

This might be particularly the case in junctures of increasing insecurity, fear, conflict, and/or violence—where life hangs by a thread and where the conditions of life of a growing segment of a population (including those accustomed to the highest positions of power and authority) are perceived as being on the brink of disaster. Dialogue, reflection, conciliation, serene negotiation, and compromise, as well as hopeful delegation and deferment, become for most unthinkable, intolerable—with perceptions of reality (knowledges) being polarized, frozen, oversimplified, and pitted against one another as part and parcel of the general climate of anxiety, when there is a need for a clear, prompt resolution, even at a very high, once inadmissible, cost.

Under such extreme conditions (which the contemporary processes of globalization and the ongoing worldwide economic and political crises make ever more likely and unpredictable), it is common for a tendency to emerge to promptly assemble, adopt, and/or cast a straightforward and hopeful vision of reality as the only true and admissible one (the only real knowledge) and concomitantly to see any and all other visions as both false and irreconcilable with "ours" (as not-knowledge, error, or deceit)— including among intellectuals linked to groups whose existence and/or power are perceived as under serious threat.

It could be further hypothesized that this is the case not only on larger collective planes (e.g., nations, regions) but also at the microsocial stage (e.g., neighborhoods, families, classrooms, churches), as well as at the individual level.

Individuals experiencing radical insecurity (because of, for example, a job loss, the death of a loved one, foreclosure on their home, the onset of a fatal illness, a serious accident, a destructive addiction, a marital breakup, or violence at the hands of a close partner or relative) might be more open to a radical change of their perception of reality, including embracing forms of knowledge hitherto unacceptable to them—and to taking these up in a much more vigorous, closed, aggressive, and defensive manner than they ever embraced any other vision of reality in their past. By the same token, the way in which this embrace of new knowledge might tend to take place is by redoubling it with attempts to impose it on others, closing off any avenues for dialogue with even (formerly) loved ones, and, in the extreme, by joining in violent actions to destroy symbols or, worse, human lives, linked to those other ("false") knowledges. Think, among other things, of the bombings of abortion clinics, the assassination of Freedom Riders in the 1960s, that of Matthew Shepard, the rape and murder of the four religious women in El Salvador on December 2, 1980, and the 9/11 attacks in the United States—but think no less of the discomfort some would feel when seeing all these cases lumped together.

Neighborhoods and small groups and/or families within neighborhoods, whose lives, traditions, expectations, and safety are growingly menaced by drug dealers, shootouts, police violence, unemployment, and/or city attempts to renovate their area (with the consequent, usually definitive, relocation of residents and disintegration of the community), might similarly develop or embrace ways of looking at their world that could at times shift into closed, intolerant, even violent forms of defending and imposing one's own truth. Think of youth gangs, Pentecostal churches, and petitions for the eviction of undocumented immigrants in several places in contemporary New Jersey—and, again, of the possible discomfort of some readers that these things are placed on the same level.

However, whereas such a tendency to brandish under duress one's own old or new knowledge as exclusive truth might translate into thriving strategies of consensus building and self-preservation among the elites (who actually do very often have the material and symbolic resources to spread and enforce a certain vision of the world while restraining most, if not all, other competing visions—as shown worldwide in recent decades with the global embrace, from tabloids to graduate schools of economics, of the neoliberal fundamentalism of the invisible hand and free markets), tragically, this is rarely the case among the subaltern.

What most often takes place among disadvantaged, vulnerable, marginalized groups under duress (precisely because their social location entails, among other things, the scarcity of material and symbolic resources to spread and enforce a certain vision of the world while restraining most other competing visions) is the multiplication of competing knowledge claims and knowledge authorities—many indigenous, many imported, and most a creative synthesis of both local and extraneous elements—hardly able to sustain the onslaught from above and from the outside, the bitter antagonisms generated by the climate and available options, and/or the hard labor required to maintain and prolong credibility, outreach, cohesion, and effective mobilization. Thus, the emergence of new knowledge under duress among the subaltern is constantly threatened with disintegration and co-optation, and it is prone more often than not to bring forth in the long run self-destructive developments—rather than the purported opposite aim of furthering new knowledge(s).

Paradoxically, the affordable luxuries, in Western democracies at least, that self-criticism and critical analysis constitute, in general, for middle-class professionals and intellectuals—luxuries that can actually enhance, rather than threaten, their recognition and prestige among peers and the larger public—probably constitute among the subaltern a much more urgent component, albeit less affordable, for the production, distribution, exchange, and transformation of new knowledges, precisely to offset the (constant, inevitable) tendency to shape new knowledge(s) as closed, absolute, exclusive truths, alongside the building of a "new epistemological order" (e.g., that of Marxism, "national Catholicism," liberation theology,

Zionism, Shiite Islam, National Socialism, or Pentecostalism), which might easily end up—at a smaller or larger scale—birthing new, destructive dynamics and structures of oppression within, or instead of, the dominant ones.

V

As suggested by the recent tradition of popular education (since Paulo Freire), it is not only (and possibly not mainly, except rarely) through the actual content of a discourse or utterance (written, sung, spoken, iconic, gestured, or otherwise) that its most significant meanings are transmitted, disseminated, and/or reinforced. Equally or possibly more important in transmitting knowledge is the form of the transmission, including the actual relations between the "vessels" of knowledge (e.g., speaker, book, song, image, sensation) and the audience experiencing, perceiving the utterances expressed by and/or through the "vessel." The forms through which we express our knowledge (e.g., linear, "logical," academic prose) can be, in and of themselves, ways of knowing, of normalizing certain ways of knowing, of authorizing certain authorities, and—at least by omission—of delegitimating, obliterating, and/or silencing other ways of knowing, different sources of knowledge, multiple forms of expressing knowledge, and, beyond, entire cultures, regions, and traditions involving far more numerous and diverse populations (and their millennia of histories) than those represented in, privy to, and involved in the dominant ways of knowing our world.

Thus, an authoritarian form of transmission of knowledge—as in scholarly lectures, ceremonial speeches, or religious homilies, where interruptions, challenges, and questions are a priori out of order—might serve to confirm and reinforce a self-perception of oneself and one's peers as incapable of being a speaker. Such effect is frequently redoubled by a confirmation of the superiority of the speakers and their (class, gender, linguistic, ethnic, racial, and/or educational) peers, particularly when the traits of most of those occupying the positions of discursive authority are not just consistently repeated across times and places but are also constantly different from those of the segments of the population finding themselves and their peers almost invariably in the location of passive receptors, followers, believers (e.g., students, readers, hearers, audience) of authoritative discourses.

This effect of the form in which knowledge is presented and transmitted can easily offset or outweigh any and all antiauthoritarian intentions and contents in the spokesperson(s) and/or her, his, or their ideas. In other words, "new" knowledges, or supposed "counter-knowledges," depending, among other things, on the form in which they are expressed and transmitted, could in fact transmit and induce a reinforcement of, rather than a challenge to, dominant ideas, groups, relations, and practices. Think, for instance, of authoritarian, rigid, top-down teachers teaching their students "socialist" ideas and making clear that whoever responds to exam questions with unacceptable, contrary ideas will indeed flunk their course—or worse.

Conversely, a democratic, dialogical, horizontal, nonthreatening, welcoming, inclusive, egalitarian form of presenting and discussing "conservative" ideas could elicit discussions, reflection, research, and exchanges of opinions among participants, leading at least some of them to generate critiques and alternatives to the ideas originally presented, and/or to bring forth interpretations of such ideas, which, rather than reinforcing domineering and dominant practices and relations, might foster a novel, transformative, "progressive" take. Think, for instance, of the turn that many evangelicals, especially young ones, have recently taken in relation to hunger, poverty, homelessness, immigrants, and the environment.

The printed word as a privileged vehicle of knowledge (including as a surreptitious propaganda device to consecrate certain forms of knowledge, certain knowledges, and certain knowers while devaluing others) presents its own kind of epistemological problems, not only insofar as it has the capacity to spread certain content widely, but also, even more significant, as a culturally overdetermined form that, almost in and of itself (again regardless of its actual content or the intentions of its users), evokes and buttresses a certain idea of where and/or how worthy knowledge is expressed (in printed prose, like this one), where and/or how authorized knowers present worthy knowledge (in published books and journals—but not in any nor all books or journals), and what true knowledge looks like (in "stable" print form, transmissible, somewhat "always same," with a supposedly fixed meaning and appearance).

All the above are likely to be more probable if and when producers and/or transmitters of knowledge and those "receiving" it are not only different but when their relations are unequal, imbalanced, lopsided power relations, or, worse, relations of oppression, exclusion, domination, and exploitation. Thus, the content of a discourse critical of asymmetrical relations (e.g., class relations between industry shareholders and manual workers in the same industry), in which the critic happens to be located in a position closer to the privileged pole of the relations, can be grasped in radically opposite ways by audiences closer to one or the other pole in such relations—for instance, as intolerably subversive by the critic's peers and as one more empty gesture of superficial sympathy by those in the weaker end of the relation.

Knowing as women, African Americans, lesbian and gay people, Hispanics, Native Americans, Asian Americans, or persons with disabilities— even when explicitly and deliberately resisting, denouncing, fighting, and subverting oppression—is knowing not just beyond and against oppression, but it is also, always, knowing under and from within oppression, and thus it is a knowing immensely more prone to, tempted by, and liable to being co-opted, swallowed, digested, and excreted, as it were, by the very same relations of oppression under, within, and against which such "counter-knowledge from below" emerges. And such an occurrence is all the more possible because it can develop without one's knowledge or will, all the more so if and/or when such counter-knowledge is produced without a consistent, deliberate, continuous effort to pinpoint and fight the very tendencies and enticements to fall back into the dominant ways of knowing while honestly thinking we are continuing to produce a genuine counter-knowledge.

VI

A claim to know, to have knowledge, to know where knowledge is, how to get it, and who has it is more and other and more perilous than just an intellectual claim. Such epistemological claims mobilize appetites, hopes, and fears. They might reactivate, reanimate, reawaken dormant memories, worries, patterns, and desires, and thus mobilize people toward or away from certain groups, thoughts, courses of action, and reflection— regardless of, and also over against, the best intentions of those (re)introducing certain knowledge claims in a particular juncture of a group's history.

VII

Globalization accelerates, multiplies, and elicits the constant crisscrossing, encounters, conflicts, clashes, and mutual influences and transformations of a multiplicity of knowledges, knowers, and ways of knowing—often unevenly able to deal openly and creatively with each other. Dialogue and syncretisms are only a few of the dynamics emerging from these encounters, sadly often overshadowed (or worse) by destructive dynamics of invisibility, denial, exclusion, persecution, (in)civil wars, and other forms of conflict generated in the encounter among diverse ways of knowing through migrations, seasonal labor, maquiladoras, electronic communications, and other dimensions of the contemporary processes of globalization.

VIII

The paradox of a way of knowing that aims to undermine an authoritarian, hierarchical, exploitive social system is that, in order not to mimic, legitimate, and serve as an instrument of that very system, it needs to shape itself as an open, humble, dialogical, consistently self-examining way of understanding and producing knowledge—which inevitably turns it into a more fragile, vulnerable way of understanding and producing knowledge, even more liable to be destroyed by the very social system it emerges against.

IX

All epistemological problems are simultaneously political and ethical problems. All political problems are simultaneously ethical and epistemological problems. All ethical problems are simultaneously political and epistemological problems. Actual power dynamics, our efforts toward knowledge, and our accountability toward our planet and all our fellow creatures are intricately intertwined with one another.

X

The dangerous ideal of a universal, eternal, and singular true knowledge—a delusion that is habitually part of imperial designs of forced unification, subjection, and homogenization of a variety of ways of being human—is all too often one of the most intractable hurdles to the peaceful resolution of human conflicts, to the respect and flourishing of human diversity, and to the possibility of learning from such conflicts and diversity a few new and better ways of coexisting with one another. Would it be socially think-able to humbly and respectfully launch, at a fairly broad and durable scale, an invitation to reach partial, temporary, open agreements as to the variety of (epistemological) knowledges, (ethical) values, and (political) structures within which we can live—and within which we can revise, transform, and disagree, too, on the variety of acceptable ways of living? Would it be feasible to start among some US Latina/o groupings an experiment in epistemological, ethical, and political humility that becomes someday a witness of another way not just of knowing but of knowing justly: know-ing in a way that contributes to enhancing life on earth for all?

❧ Migrants' Religions under Imperial Duress: Reflections on Epistemology, Ethics, and Politics in the Study of the Religious "Stranger"

PRESIDENTIAL ADDRESS 2012
AMERICAN ACADEMY OF RELIGION, CHICAGO, 2012

PRELIMINARY REMARKS

Scientific knowledge in general—and religious studies in particular—are nowadays carried out in a global cultural environment where concern and compassion toward the vulnerable, the weak, the victims of violence and marginalization, are increasingly devalued as impractical weaknesses, whereas indifference, callousness, and insensitivity in their regard seem to become the new objectivity, the new scientificity, the new normalcy—including in religious discourse and public policy.

In this address, I want to invite us to reflect on the need to appreciate and explore the complex interconnections between (1) our ways of knowing, of determining what and how is worth knowing, of judging and using knowledge and expertise (*epistemology*); (2) our values, priorities, and urgencies (*ethics*); and (3) the power structures, dynamics, allegiances, and interests in which we are involved and which bound our knowledge and our ethics (*politics*)—and how these interconnections orient and shape, among other things, our perceptions of the "other," the alien, the stranger, and their religious ways.

This invitation is made while underscoring the increasingly inimical environment where immigrants to the United States find themselves after 9/11—and even more so since the current financial crisis burst out: an environment where evictions, detentions, workplace raids, late-night home searches, job firings, school expulsions, forced family separations, police abuse, posse attacks, deportations, denial of services, homelessness, discrimination of all sorts, and the deep fears this all raises, are progressively becoming part and parcel of the daily lives of immigrants, especially poor, recent, undocumented, dark-skinned, non-English-speaking immigrants; an environment where religious traditions and faith communities are carried on with a novel urgency and vulnerability.

I am indeed honored and grateful for having been nominated and elected to the presidency of the AAR [American Academy of Religion]—and thus having the opportunity to deliver this year its presidential address. When asked about what "power" does the AAR president have, I often answer that—besides one of twelve votes in our board, one of six in its Executive Committee, and the nomination and appointment of some of our colleagues to certain posts in our organization—in the end, the only power we AAR presidents have is the "power" of crafting and uttering our presidential address. The little power AAR presidents have—and maybe that is a good thing in many respects—has been evident in the difficulties encountered this year to respond positively to the calls of the hotel workers' union to support their boycott of the Hyatt chain. It seems we don't even have quite the power to title our presidential address. In your program you will find as its title what was originally its subtitle, "Reflections on Epistemology, Ethics, and Politics in the Study of the Religious 'Stranger.'" Somewhere along the process of readying our annual program, the title of the address (and the theme of our 2012 annual meetings, too) was lost: it was actually "Migrants' Religions under Imperial Duress." Allow me to make that title explicit before entering into the subject matter of this address.

INTRODUCTION

Let me start with a quote from Max Weber:

> The primary task of a useful teacher is to teach his students to recognize "inconvenient" facts—I mean facts that are inconvenient for their party opinions. And for every party opinion there are facts that are extremely inconvenient, for my own opinion no less than for others.[1]

Our most well-intentioned actions often result in outcomes that are quite contrary to the goals of our actions. I recall here an interview that appeared a couple of years ago in the pages of Drew University's student newspaper, *The Acorn*. It dealt with the labor policies of the corporation that subcontracted the grounds, food, and cleaning services at our university. It zeroed in, specifically, on the pervasive policy of hiring undocumented laborers for the lowest possible salary and firing them on the spot and without compensation whenever issues arose with immigration authorities. A picture of two of the Latina women who served food in our university dining hall illustrated the well-meaning, well-written report. These two women, who had been working for several years in our campus, were fired the next day—no explanations given.

When I directed and carried on a research—back in 2000, and then again in 2007—on the hundred-odd Latina/o Pentecostal congregations that have flourished in the city of Newark, New Jersey, one of the rites that most deeply impressed me in some of these churches were precisely the rites of welcoming back undocumented Hispanic workers from, and sending them forth back home, across the southwestern border between Mexico and the United States, alongside prayers for the sick, the unemployed, and those in prison. This was right before the upsurge in deportations of the last four years (near one million deportees in these last four years, according to reliable sources), deportations which have shattered the lives, dreams, and families of a growing, colossal number of members of Latina/o communities and churches across the United States.

Scientific knowledge in general, including religious studies, are human efforts carried out in our times amid a global cultural environment where concern for, compassion toward, and solidarity with the vulnerable, the persecuted, the victims of violence and marginalization, are all increasingly devalued as extrascientific worries, impractical weaknesses which get in the way of objectivity, impartiality, and the like, whereas indifference, coldness, and "neutrality" in their regard, seem to become the new objectivity, the new scientificity, the new normalcy—including in the study of religion, in religious discourse itself, as well as in public policy.

In this address, I want to invite us to reflect on the need to appreciate and explore the complex interconnections among the following dimensions:

1. Our ways of knowing, of determining what and how is worth knowing, of judging and using knowledge and expertise (*epistemology*)
2. Our values, priorities, and urgencies (*ethics*)

3. The power structures, dynamics, allegiances, and interests in which we are involved and which bound both our knowledge and our ethics (*politics*)—and how these interconnections orient and shape, among others, our perceptions of the other, the alien, the stranger, and their religious ways

1. KNOWLEDGE, VALUES, AND POWER

Truth is not born nor is it to be found inside the head of an individual person, it is born between people collectively searching for truth, in the process of their dialogic interaction.[2]

A certain understanding of Max Weber, which I would claim is in fact a distortion of his thought, casts scientific knowledge as "value neutral," and Weber as its champion. Against this conception, and with a significantly different interpretation of Weber's idea of scientific knowledge, I would submit that what Weber offers is a much more complex, interesting, and difficult call than what hides behind the idea of scientific knowledge as "value-free." For starters, Weber is convinced that our values, desires, interests, fears, et cetera, indeed influence and shape our scientific investigations—our choices of topics, foci, variables, methods, partners, assumptions, approaches, and, often, of interpretations of collected data. We are neither passive nor innocent data collectors. Inspiration, preferences, and presuppositions all plague what becomes visible and what is rendered invisible throughout our scientific research. Or, as Weber himself put it in his 1897 essay "'Objectivity' in Social Science and Social Policy,"

> A chaos of "existential judgments" about countless individual events would be the only result of a serious attempt to analyze reality "without presuppositions." . . . Order is brought into this chaos only on the condition that in every case only a *part* of concrete reality is interesting and *significant* to us, because it is related to the *cultural values* with which we approach reality.[3]

What Weber therefore proposes on the part of the researchers is a constant effort to discern which *values*, preferences, desires, fears, allegiances, et cetera, are in fact shaping their research and how—so that researchers become gradually abler to detect, monitor, and decide, in view of the values that they consciously choose to embrace and deliberately want to serve with their research, to what degree the course and results of their research owes more to their subjective wishes than to a careful assessment of the realities in place. In this sense, a "value-free" scientific research, rather than an unquestionable fact or an ethical obligation of the scientist, is a regulative ideal[4] in the Kantian sense—or, to use mathematical jargon, an asymptotic process to which the scientist is invited by Max Weber: something never fully attainable, constantly evading us, but which we can get at times closer and closer to, as long as we constantly strive to achieve it.

With and beyond Weber, I would submit that there is a double ethical challenge here: on one hand, that of unveiling and critically examining the values that actually, but most often unconsciously, in fact guide our research, and, on the other hand, the challenge of choosing which values do we consciously want to actually serve with our research without letting them push us, as it were, to conclusions that are not warranted by actual, well-researched facts.

This challenge to scientific research—including, of course, social-scientific research on religious phenomena—becomes more difficult and complex when we recognize our knowledge and our ethics as deeply enmeshed in, and fashioned by, too, the lopsided *power* relations and power dynamics that characterize our contemporary societies, that involve us, traverse our research enterprises, and comprise the very subjects of our scientific pursuits, too.

Such an acknowledgment raises and includes the ethical challenge, too, of our status as recognized scholars, legitimate academics, sanctioned scientists, accredited intellectuals, and / or authorized researchers. What does such recognition, legitimation, sanction, accreditation, and authorization imply in relation to the subjects of our research—particularly when their language, garb, rites, educational trajectory, income level, social location, migratory status, dwelling place, gestures, attitudes, skin color, and / or religious affiliation place them in a significantly different—nay, an *inferior*—disadvantaged position in relation to the one we researchers occupy? How "objective" can our study of *them* be? And which interests and strategies will our research *actually* serve in relation to *them*—regardless, or even against our own best intentions and conscious efforts?

The very fact of being documented intellectuals researching undocumented religious *others* already poses, in and of itself, a political and ethical challenge to our quest for knowledge of the "religious other." We can choose to ignore it at our own risk and peril—but it is likely that our subjects of research *cannot* ignore the risks and perils to which our research exposes them.

Knowledge—including research on religions—is always both an ethical and a political task.

II. VALUES, KNOWLEDGE, AND POWER

We hide reality from our conscious minds the better to hide it from onlookers.[5]

An old friend of mine once advised me not to take too seriously what people say their values are. "Look at how they act, how they comport themselves and respond to the regular trials of daily life," he instructed me. "That's where you'll grasp what their values actually are."

We might suggest likewise in relation to ourselves as researchers on religion. It is only nor so much to honest declarations of which values we embrace, nor to intellectual accounts of the ethics of our research that we should pay attention. Rather, what is usually dodged, and I want to underscore as key for an ethical discussion here, are the actual social dynamics within which our research is intertwined, as well as the impact of our research on those same dynamics—including the real-life consequences for our research subjects.

Let us consider this possibility. We live in a global world where corporations, media, governments, universities, and international institutions (especially but not only those related to business and finances) are increasingly participating in the creation, diffusion, assumption, and daily enactment a new global ethic: one where callousness, insensitivity, indifference, and disregard for the "collateral damages" of the economic activity of global contemporary capitalism on the lives of the most vulnerable living beings (billions of humans included) are acceptable for the sake of profits, productivity, expansion, and growth—whereas care, concern, compassion, accompaniment, solidarity, and protection of the most vulnerable living beings is more and more derided and looked down upon as passé, infantile, or counterproductive when not outright evil, sinful, or criminal. We would not be at all alone in arguing that this (usually unspoken) set of assumptions progressively pervades the lives of a growing number of institutions and groups of people in our globalized world—usually starting among the urban elites but slowly impacting the lives of entire nations.

In such a context, how can research remain ethically neutral?

The issue here is not a simple one. Certainly not one of just declaring why such context is irrelevant for our research, or of morally condemning such dynamics and then pursuing our research as if the problem has thus been solved. What I would suggest, rather, is that the issue is a long-lasting one; one that will not go away with verbal statements; one that, on the contrary, requires being taken seriously through and through.

What I want to propose here, or, rather, what I want to add my voice to, is a call for taking seriously this possibility: that we, our research subjects, and our research endeavors, are all enmeshed in lopsided *power* relations and dynamics. That such relations and dynamics surreptitiously and pervasively impose limits, directions, and likely consequences to our research. That we would benefit, therefore, from a constant critical examination of both the larger context of our research—particularly in relation to its lopsided *power* relations and dynamics—and the long-term impact of the same in the individuals and communities affected, directly or indirectly, by our research. That, in brief, all ethical matters are, also, simultaneously, *power* issues, political matters.

This is all particularly timely and relevant in these times when migrants and their religions—not only in the United States, but remarkably also in the United States—are increasingly subjected to the forces of unbridled, free-market, global capitalism, to the ravages of the current economic crisis, to the natural catastrophes of global warming, to the unpredictability and insecurity that come along with these processes, to the scapegoating of undocumented nonwhite workers that emerges from such a situation of uncertainty and fear, and to the governmental policies against undocumented immigrants implemented in the last four years.

As probably in all human groupings, there are things that we do partially out of ignorance—not knowing certain things allows us to act in certain ways without second thoughts. And, because of that ignorance, we often contribute to outcomes that we do not want—outcomes that we would normally reject from the ethical perspective we embrace. But there are also many things that we do not want to know, information in front of which we prefer to look the other way, facts that we rather not face. This complex human process which we name *knowledge* is also made of ethical decisions (more often than not unconscious ones) to proactively ignore, forget, erase, and/or overlook certain aspects of our world. There are things that we don't want, things that we don't know, and things that we don't want to know—and our research and its results are shaped in large measure by such factors.

Fear is a major factor in those ethical decisions concerning the *knowledge* of our surrounding world. Fear of our own ethical responsibility regarding certain facts; fear of rejection by our colleagues and peers in the profession; fear of the consequences of such decisions for the advancement of our careers; fear of losing certain benefits, perks, connections, and privileges; fear of the responses of our loved ones, of our significant others; fear, often, in the long term, of the very same traits that affect many of the religious "others" that we study—that is, unstable jobs, unemployment, reduced health care, diminished income, inability to afford a home or to sustain one's family, food insecurity, et cetera. Fear, too, of living in fear.

Do we really want to know that there are Christian groups in the US Southwest that are committed, for religious reasons, to save the lives of border crossers by repeatedly placing or filling up water tanks and containers in the routes trod by undocumented immigrants—while, simultaneously, there are other Christian groups which, for reasons that they see as a deep part of their religious faith, poison or pierce those tanks and containers to ensure that the border crossers do not reach their goal? Do we actually want to remember that our authorities all too often look the other way, particularly in the case of the latter groups of Christians? Do we truly want to recall that these last years have seen at least one border crosser die every day before reaching their goal, either of thirst, hunger, dehydration, freezing, snake bites, or shot by *coyotes*, the *migra*, or white nativist Christian posses? Do we want to ponder the monstrousness of broken families, abandoned children, suicides, and a host of other tragedies elicited in the last four years by a government that has deported near one million immigrants—most of them hardworking, honest people who came to the United States because of the impoverishment and/or violence plaguing their homeland? Would we like to consider for a split second that such impoverishment and violence south of the border owes too much, precisely, to the economic, military, political, and cultural policies of both US governments and corporations? And that the affordability for the US middle classes of many of the staples we find in our supermarkets is but one of the advantages we enjoy thanks to those very policies? Or would we rather not let any of these "inconvenient facts" disturb our research?

And how do these questions and the related realities affect religions (the religions of the undocumented and those of the documented), and vice versa?

In any case, it would appear as if the question of ethics in relation to research on religions in our contemporary world could hardly be disentangled from the serious epistemological and political dimensions of our lives in that same world.

III. POWER, KNOWLEDGE, AND VALUES

One of the many ways in which asymmetric, lopsided, unequal power relations at any level—familiar, institutional, neighborhood, local, regional, national, or global—affect humans is precisely through their insidious effects, direct and indirect, unspoken or overt, on our perception of power relations and power dynamics themselves. The denial, trivialization, marginalization, normalization, or stigmatization of the actuality and significance of power relations and dynamics could be critically analyzed as some among multiple ways in which power relations continually reproduce themselves in our daily lives.

As Robert Trivers suggested, "We hide reality from our conscious minds the better to hide it from onlookers."

Michel Foucault was not the first, nor was he the last, either, to submit that there are a multiplicity of complex, subtle ways in which power and *knowledge* are interconnected. As the sociology of knowledge has proposed since its inception in the nineteenth century, and as it has been studied by many other disciplines since, social power includes, among other things, the power to shape the ways in which most members of a society understand and decide, for very long periods of time, what is knowledge, how to tell apart and obtain legitimate knowledge, who has the authority to decide these things and to resolve controversies about them, what is *not* legitimate knowledge (but, instead, falsehoods, illusions, lies, superstitions, biases, prejudices, et cetera), which untruths should be silenced, persecuted, punished, and eradicated—and how, when, where.

Power is not just material, physical power—the power of the strong, the power of weapons, the power of the many. Power is also what Bourdieu calls symbolic power: respect, authority, acquiescence, admiration, legitimacy, esteem, prestige, reputation, regard. That is, power is also the ability to transmute and accrue material power by subtly exacting assent, acquiescence, consent, recognition, submission—and, yes, fear. Or to put it again in Bourdieu's words, power is the capacity to produce, in oneself no less than in others, the misrecognition of the arbitrary as good, natural, inevitable, and/or sacred. In other words, power is also the power to redouble material power with what we could label "epistemological power," that is, the capacity to produce a type of knowledge that ceases to question and problematize the prevailing power arrangements, and, on the contrary, pushes us either to look away from them and/or to perceive those power arrangements as normal—not to be questioned, challenged, or opposed.

This is why talking about primitive religions, world religions, organized religions, terrorism, or violence is scientifically acceptable in certain times and places, and in reference to certain phenomena, but not in reference to other phenomena. May we ask if by any chance our regular police and other armed forces are terrorizing today significant segments of our population? Why silence is scientifically permissible or even requisite in reference to certain religious movements and as far as their relations with certain social phenomena are concerned, as was the case in Nazi Germany or Sukarno's Indonesia or Ríos Montt's Guatemala—but also in the US academic community in relation to the latter two? Could the fact that 80 percent of the African American males of certain US counties are legally hindered from voting for having been in prison have anything to do with their religious choices, beliefs, and behavior? Or are questions such as these scientifically irrelevant?

When is knowledge subversive?

It is worthy to note here that the study of sociology—including the sociology of religions—is often suspect in the eyes of those occupying positions of religious, political, military, and economic power. In the Soviet Union, Nazi Germany, Edgar Hoover's USA, as well as in the multifarious military dictatorships supported throughout the entire third world by US, Nazi or Soviet administrations, sociology in general has been repeatedly cast, investigated, persecuted, repressed, and obliterated as a suspicious, subversive endeavor. And in many religious institutions, educational and otherwise, in the United States and abroad, sociology—even more so when directed to the study of religion—has suffered a similar fate.

Does this say anything about the study of religion?

Heinrich Heine was the one to insightfully call the bible a Jewish "portable homeland." We could apply the label to all religions, particularly in the case of migrants. Migrants' religions are their portable homelands, the array of icons, texts, beliefs, rites, songs, stories, relations, and orientations that give them security, refuge, sanctuary, self-worth, hope, and stamina even when all surrounding signs are omens of destruction and terror. Homeland security? Sadly, what millions of undocumented migrant workers, sucked in by the insatiable thirst for cheap labor of large and small US corporations are experiencing—especially after 9/11 and even more so since the beginning of the global financial crisis—is mounting terror in the face of deadly racist assaults by white supremacist posses, school expulsions, denial of health and legal services, confiscation of drivers licenses, denial of insurance, late-night home invasions by security forces, workplace raids by the US Department of Homeland Security, mass incarceration of entire families with their members separated in distant facilities by gender and age but with nobody informed of their whereabouts, deportations by the hundreds of thousands, loss of jobs, of homes, of lifetime savings, of relations cultivated through decades, of years of hard labor and of resilient dreams of a better life for their children.

What more is needed to make this terrorizing trend a national, public moral issue? More corpses per day? More migrant cadavers in the daily news?

And, let me suggest, in these dire circumstances, it is often only religious congregations—especially those founded by migrants, with migrants, for migrants—that are left to care for the "collateral damages" of national xenophobia, white supremacy, and nativism.

How do we know these migrants' religions under imperial duress? What do we know of them? How do we study them, what for, and with which consequences? How does their current predicament challenge our views, our methods, and our research?

As intellectuals, we brandish a special kind of power. How do we use that power, with whom, for whom, what for?

Power is an *ethical* issue. And it is a more urgent ethical issue when human lives are at stake, when innocent children's lives are at stake—not just occasionally and in small numbers, but repeatedly, increasingly so, and in the hundreds of thousands.

Power is thus not just a political matter: it is an ethical and an epistemological issue as well, and inextricably so.

AN INVITATION AS PROVISIONAL CONCLUSION

This invitation is made while underscoring the ever more inimical environment where immigrants to the United States find themselves after 9/11—and even more so since the current financial crisis burst out. This environment of mounting fear is progressively becoming part and parcel of the daily lives of immigrants, especially poor, recent, undocumented, dark-skinned, non-English-speaking immigrants; an environment where religious traditions and faith communities are carried on with a novel urgency and vulnerability.

This is, among others, an invitation to consider religion as that social space where it is discussed—and decisions are made in this regard—whose lives are sacred, worthy of care and concern, and whose lives, on the contrary, are disposable, sacrificible, irrelevant, and who is to make such judgments, where, and how.

This is an urgent invitation for us as researchers, teachers, academics, scholars of religion—but also as plain citizens and simple human beings—to hear the cry of the oppressed and to respond to that cry, with our power, our ethical responsibility, and our role in the production and dissemination of knowledge, in any and all forms within our reach.

Thank you.

NOTES

INTRODUCTION TO THE ENGLISH-LANGUAGE EDITION

1. I have retained the "Latina/o" inflection that Otto Maduro used in his own translation. This is one of the purest forms of Spanglish that reveals the extent to which Latina/os have impacted U.S. culture, percolating even into English vernacular. Evidently, the expression is based on neither Spanish nor English grammar. Here is linguistic *mestizaje*. It is the result of the attempt to make English, a language that effaces gender from its grammar, speak like Spanish, a language that is thoroughly suffused by gendered nouns, pronouns, and adjectives. "Latina/o" is retained when it refers to Latinos in general, who would be either male or female. I have opted for "Latino" when it evidently refers to Otto Maduro, as the subject of many sentences, in which Otto was expressing his singularly Latino perspective, which was a male, Latina/o, perspective. In that case, the "o" is most apropos.

2. Jorge Luis Borges, *A Universal History of Infamy*, trans. Norman Thomas di Giovanni (New York: E. P. Dutton, 1970).

3. Jerry Brotton, *A History of the World in 12 Maps* (New York: Viking, 2013).

4. Miranda Fricker, *Epistemic Injustice: Power and the Ethics of Knowing* (Oxford: Oxford University Press, 2007).

5. Robert N. Proctor and Londa Schiebinger, *Agnotology: The Making and Unmaking of Ignorance* (Stanford, CA: Stanford University Press, 2008).

6. Shannon Sullivan and Nancy Tuana, eds., *Race and the Epistemologies of Ignorance* (Albany: State University of New York Press, 2007).

7. Ernst Bloch, *Natural Law and Human Dignity*, trans. Dennis J. Schmidt (Cambridge, MA: MIT Press, 1986).

INTRODUCTION

1. Rubem Alves, *Estórias de quem gosta de ensinar* (São Paulo: Cortez Editora-Autores Asociados, 1984), 21 and 43. Translations by author.

2. See Otto Maduro, "Avertissements épistémologico-politiques pour une sociologie latino-américaine des religions," in *Social Compass* (Leuven, Belgium) 26, nos. 2–3 (1979): 179–94.

3. [The Maryknoll School of Theology was closed in 1994 because of a lack of financial resources. —*Ed.*]

4. Besides the more than two hundred students who contributed to these reflections (hard to list them!), I should mention, among others, my 1991–92 colleagues at CESEP, Regina Soares Jurkewicz, Pepita Buendía, Julio de Santa Ana, Hans Börn, Luciano Glavina, and José Oscar Beozzo; and at ISER-Asessoria, Ivo Lesbaupin, Pedro Ribeiro de Oliveira, Paulo Fernando Carneiro de Andrade, Faustino Teixeira, Solange dos Santos Rodrigues, Clodovis Boff, Lúcia Ribeiro, Névio Florin, and Rogério Valle.

1. DOES EXPERIENCE SHAPE OUR KNOWLEDGE?

1. Among the best books that I know that develops this thesis is Jean Piaget's *Biology and Knowledge: An Essay on the Relation between Organic Regulations and Cognitive Processes*, trans. Beatrix Walsh (Chicago: University of Chicago Press, 1971).

2. That is the true *popular* sense, in my view, of the democratic institutions such as freedom of thought, speech, press, association, political organization, nomination of candidates, votes, recall of public functionaries, and so on. Without these freedoms—which is what many of us understand as dictatorship—the abuse of power is facilitated (military, civil, capitalist, socialites, or whatever it may be). All of this profoundly affects what is understood in a society as *knowledge* and what is rejected and persecuted as *error*. Perhaps therein lies the explanation of what happened to Marxism in the experiments of Eastern Europe and why those experiments they fell.

3. I had a similar experience with the daughters from my first marriage. After the failures and contradictions of six pediatricians and two healers, the ninth doctor was forced for this reason to doubt his knowledge and "discover" what they had: mucoviscidosis, or cystic fibrosis (an incurable genetic disease). Both died: Jenny at two, in 1971; Vanessa at three, in 1974. This experience most certainly led me to change my views about life and knowledge. This book, in more than one sense, is the fruit of that experience.

4. It seems to me that this hypothesis, though initially developed in relation to the modern and explicit Western scientific theories, would be interesting to

expand in order to address any more or less structured image of reality—scientific, modern, occidental, explicit. Or perhaps not! Among the best books I know in which a similar idea is developed—and from which I took it—is Paul K. Feyerabend's *Against Method* (London: Verso, 1988). For Feyerabend, in fact, the "advancement" of an old scientific theory to a new one is fruit precisely of such contradictions.

5. This is no longer directly practiced by Christian churches as such; it was practiced at least until the nineteenth century in most regions under Christian control, including the nineteenth-century Americas (see, for example, the movies of *The Scarlet Letter* and *The Crucible*). Today, members of many churches—acting from governments or paramilitary groups in alleged defense of the faith—still practice this form knowledge control. As an example, the Guatemalan military dictatorship of General Efraín Ríos Montt, was presented on several US television channels as "the first Christian government in history."

2. CALMLY REFLECTING ON OUR KNOWLEDGE

1. All of the new feminist epistemology that has been developing in the past decades, above all in the United States, departs in some way, it seems to me, from this perspective. In any event, my proposals owes a lot to my readings of this current. See especially Mary Field Belenky, Blythe McVicker Clinchy, Nancy Rule Goldberger, and Jill Mattuck Tarule, *Women's Ways of Knowing: The Development of Self, Voice, and Mind* (New York: Basic Books, 1986).

2. From the beginning of the twentieth century, famous names of contemporary physicists—such as Werner Heisenberg and Albert Einstein, for example—have insisted that what the natural sciences measure is not an external "object" to the "subject" that knows, but the *relation* between both: between a subject affected by an object, and vice versa. In contrast, the boastful imputation—constructed out of a naive idolatry of the mathematical-physical and biochemical sciences—that the social sciences are in reality prescientific has been questioned by the hypothesis that the "exact and natural" sciences find themselves still, and very frequently, in a state of presociological and ahistorical naïveté.

3. If there is a science in which we find a great variety of opinions to such degree, it is economics . In the face of the economic crisis of the 1990s, for instance, the US conservative economists have an incredible diversity of opinions with respect to the nature and causes, the when and how the crisis developed, and why, and whence it leads, and the possible remedies in the short, medium, and long terms in order to get out of it. It is enough to read the texts and declarations of the secretary of the Treasury of presidents Reagan, Bush, and Clinton

to confirm this. Read, for example, on Joseph E. Stiglitz, chair of the Council of Economic Advisers from 1995 to 1997, and the chief economist of the World Bank in 1998, the article by Louis Uchitelle, "The Economics of Intervention," *New York Times*, Money and Business, May 31, 1998.

4. Some Brazilian friends told me that there is a popular refrain that says, "All unanimity is asinine." In this general field of ideas a US intellectual said that "when the whole world thinks the same, no one is really thinking."

5. [Otto Maduro intended to include a note inviting readers to directly send to him criticisms or suggestions for improving the manuscript. He intended to include his email and address. He wrote, "Although I cannot promise detailed individualized responses, I do promise to read closely and respectfully any correspondence, and I will take seriously whatever is suggested and I will try at the very least to acknowledge its receipt." —*Ed.*]

3. OPPRESSION, LIBERATION, AND KNOWLEDGE

1. [The PRI was defeated electorally in the 2000 election, when Vicente Fox, candidate from the Partido de Acción Nacional (PAN) was elected to the presidency. —*Ed.*]

2. Gifford Pinchot III, "Americano critica ação estatal," Negócios, *Jornal do Brasil* (Rio de Janeiro), October 4, 1991. Similar ideas have been expressed many times by, among others, Michael Novak, a US neoconservative Catholic intellectual, acerbic critic of the Latin American theology of liberation.

3. It is already more than a century that the more advanced theorists of physics (Heisenberg and Einstein, among others) have been insisting that human knowledge is not a passive capture—purely "cerebral"—of reality, but rather an active intervention that modifies reality and that consequently it does not allow us to speak of reality independent of human knowledge, nor of an abstractly objective knowledge.

4. "Ação do quinino é revelada depois de séculos de uso," *Jornal do Brasil* (Rio de Janeiro), January 22, 1992.

5. According to research by John Wennberg, of the Dartmouth School of Medicine, only "about half of the 230,000 operations (or coronary bypass) done in the United States had an unequivocal indication." ("Estudo nos EUA revela má prática da medicina," *Jornal do Brasil* [Rio de Janeiro], December 10, 1991.) Similar research reveals that more than half—90 percent according to Vicky Hufnagel, a specialist from California—of the seven hundred thousand hysterectomies carried out annually in the United States are either unnecessary or, worse, counterproductive.

6. This way of conceiving the relationship between knowledge and practical context has been commonly associated with the Anglo-Saxon philosophical school of pragmatism. Charles S. Peirce, George Herbert Mead, William James, and John Dewey are generally considered the main figures of contemporary pragmatism of the English language. Anthony Blasi has made me see that Thorstein Veblen and Charles Wright Mills applied pragmatism as a criterion of a social ethics (Veblen by distinguishing between parasitic and productive classes; Mills by judging sociological knowledge in terms of its utility in helping us liberate ourselves from certain "traps"). Marx, in some way, represents a leftist pragmatism, where revolutionary praxis is the criterion of knowledge. (Many will be shocked by this approximation, especially those Marxists in whose language—such as Spanish and Portuguese—the word *pragmatism* has so many negative connotations.)

4. HOW DO WE EXPRESS AND SHARE KNOWLEDGE?

1. Maurice Leenhardt, the European anthropologist, studied how a Melanesian culture created a new term—*Do kamo*—to express a new experience (the experience of the individual "I," and experience provoked and evoked unconsciously and continuously by language and the conduct of teachers, priests, anthropologists, police, and other Western authorities). See his book *Do Kamo: Person and Myth in the Melanesian World*, trans. Basia Miller Gulati (Chicago: University of Chicago Press, 1979).

2. It should be noted, in this sense, how in the past decades the production of texts about nonverbal communication, corporal expression, and so on, has grown.

3. It seems to me that great part of the efforts of the adult literacy movement established by Paulo Freire—which is known as consciousness raising, liberation pedagogy, or pedagogy of the oppressed—goes directly in this direction.

4. [The Sandinistas were defeated during the 1990 election, when Violeta Barrios de Chamorro was elected president of Nicaragua. The Sandinistas, however, returned to power in the 2006 election, when Daniel Ortega was elected president. —*Ed.*]

5. This phenomenon is graver and deeper than what it appears to be at first blush, and it has been analyzed and denounced each time with greater force in the last decades, from the camp of philosophy and linguistics (e.g., Michel Foucault, Luce Irigaray, Noam Chomsky), through anthropology and theology (e.g., James Cone, Elisabeth Schüssler-Fiorenza), to sociology and the political sciences (e.g., Carol Gilligan, Immanuel Wallerstein). It has been most due to

the feminist, African American, and Native American studies movements that this preoccupation has become more pressing and become more relevant.

5. RETHINKING OUR UNDERSTANDING OF KNOWLEDGE

1. And the word *science* used to be habitually taken to be synonymous with *philosophy*, as it used to be the case in German (with the words *wissen*, "to know," and *Wissenschaft*, "to busy oneself with knowing") and in Dutch (*wijzen* and *wijsbegeerte*, with similar senses to those in German, only that *wijsbegeerte* means, still today, something similar to "philosophy").

2. See the classic text by Thomas S. Kuhn, *The Structure of Scientific Revolutions*, 3rd ed. (Chicago: University of Chicago Press, 1996).

3. See his book *Against Method* (1975; London: Verso, 1988), which has been a source of inspiration for me from 1977 until the elaboration of these reflections.

4. It has already been decades, as I noted earlier, that physicists have suggested that there is no way to know reality without modifying it in some way (which is why every knowledge is of an already modified reality by knowledge itself) and that what we know is always the *relation* of an observer with what is observed—not objects separated from subjects. Unfortunately, what usually passes for science today in schools, newspapers, and magazines is far from this.

CONCLUSIONS

1. [The situation in Latin America since the turn of the twenty-first century has changed markedly. There are now some left-democratic governments that have began substantive economic policies to reverse the neoliberal agenda of the past three decades of the twentieth century. —*Ed.*]

2. Antonio Machado, *Campos de Castilla* [Fields of Castile], trans. Stanley Appelbaum (New York: Dover Publications, 2007).

3. Robin George Collingwood, *The Idea of History* (Oxford, UK: Clarendon Press, 1946).

APPENDIX A

1. The works of Karl Marx and Friedrich Engels, particularly those collected in *The Marx-Engels Reader*, ed. Robert C. Tucker, 2nd ed. (New York: W. W. Norton, 1978), constitute the point of departure of most (including my) approaches to knowledge as a social construction both shaped by, and fulfilling significant functions in, asymmetric power dynamics.

Karl Mannheim's *Ideology and Utopia: An Introduction to the Sociology of Knowledge*, trans. Edward Shils, preface by Louis Wirth (San Diego, CA: Harvest Books/Harcourt, 1985), and Peter L. Berger and Thomas Luckmann's *The Social Construction of Reality: A Treatise in the Sociology of Knowledge* (reprint; Garden City, NY: Anchor Books/Doubleday, 1990) went deeper into the analysis of human knowledge as a social product and its relations to conflictual power arrangements.

Maligned or misunderstood when not simply forgotten, especially among English-speaking social theorists right and left, Max Weber's *The Methodology of the Social Sciences*, ed. and trans. Edward A. Shils and Henry A. Finch, with a foreword by E. A. Shils (New York: Free Press, 1949), is a key point of reference for an examination of human knowledge as both a social outcome and a social instrument.

For anybody who is familiar with the work of Pierre Bourdieu, its influence will be more than evident throughout the lines of this essay. A sociologist, anthropologist, and philosopher anchored in, among other things, the Marxist, the Weberian, and the Durkheimian traditions, using each to complement and criticize the other two, Bourdieu's could be called a critical sociological epistemology: he was convinced of the essential role of lopsided power dynamics in shaping human knowledge, "individual" as well as collective, no less than of the decisive weight of acquired, shared, "legitimate" knowledges in the understanding of, participation in, and limitations for changing social inequalities. Among Pierre Bourdieu's most important writings for this endeavor at hand are *The Craft of Sociology: Epistemological Preliminaries*, with Jean-Claude Chamboredon and Jean-Claude Passeron, ed. Beate Krais, trans. Richard Nice (Berlin: Walter de Gruyter, 1991); *An Invitation to Reflexive Sociology*, with Loïc J. D. Wacquant (Chicago: University of Chicago Press, 1992); *Distinction: A Social Critique of the Judgement of Taste*, trans. Richard Nice (Cambridge, MA: Harvard University Press, 1984); *Outline of a Theory of Practice*, 2nd ed. (Cambridge: Cambridge University Press, 1977); "The Social Space and the Genesis of Groups," *Theory and Society* 14, no. 6 (1985): 723–44; Pierre Bourdieu, "Forms of Capital," in *Handbook of Theory and Research for the Sociology of Education*, ed. John G. Richardson (New York: Greenwood Press, 1986), 241–58; *Language and Symbolic Power* (Cambridge, MA: Harvard University Press, 1991); "Legitimation and Structured Interests in Weber's Sociology of Religion," in *Rationality and Modernity*, ed. Scott Lash and Sam Whirmster (London: Allen and Unwin, 1987), 119–36; and "Genesis and Structure of the Religious Field," *Comparative Social Research*, no. 13 (1991): 1–44, among many other works.

Other significant contributions to a more complex understanding of human knowledge as a biopsychosocial product are to be found, on the one hand, in the works of Jean Piaget, particularly his *Biology and Knowledge: An Essay* on the Relations between Organic Regulations and Cognitive Processes, trans. Beatrix Walsh (Chicago: University of Chicago Press, 1971), and, on the other, in the "antipsychiatry" movement, especially in some of the works of Ronald D. Laing, in which human perception is intriguingly scrutinized in its linkages to family systems, emotional development, and so on: The Politics of Experience, and, The Bird of Paradise (Harmondsworth, UK: Penguin, 1967); The Politics of the Family and Other Essays (New York: Pantheon Books, 1971); The Divided Self: An Existential Study in Sanity and Madness (London: Routledge, 1999); Sanity, Madness, and the Family: Families of Schizophrenics (London: Routledge, 1999); Self and Others (London: Routledge, 1999); Do You Love Me? An Entertainment in Conversation and Verse (New York: Pantheon Books, 1976); and Knots (London: Routledge, 1999).

Two key anthropological works on the social-cultural construction of the self have also marked my epistemological views. They are Marcel Mauss's "A Category of the Human Mind: The Notion of Person," trans. W. D. Halls, in The Category of the Person: Anthropology, Philosophy, History, ed. Michael Carrithers, Steven Collins, and Steven Lukes (Cambridge: Cambridge University Press, 1985), 1–25, and his disciple Maurice Leenhardt's Do Kamo: Person and Myth in the Melanesian World, trans. Basia Miller Gulati, with a preface by Vincent Crapanzano (Chicago: University of Chicago Press, 1979).

The philosophy and history of science have yielded important works enriching and broadening the reflection on human knowledge as both an artifact and a factor of social, historical, and cultural power dynamics. Noteworthy here are Paul Feyerabend's Against Method, 3rd ed. (London: Verso/New Left Books, 1993) and Thomas S. Kuhn's The Structure of Scientific Revolutions, 3rd ed. (Chicago: University of Chicago Press, 1996). I think worthwhile reading in this area include the works of Fritjof Capra, especially Uncommon Wisdom: Conversations with Remarkable People (Toronto: Bantam Books, 1989) and The Tao of Physics: An Exploration of the Parallels between Modern Physics and Eastern Mysticism, 4th ed. (Boston: Shambhala, 2000), and the works of Karl Popper, maybe starting with his Unended Quest: An Intellectual Biography (Glasgow: Fontana/Collins, 1976).

Likewise, the epistemological concerns of the British philosophy of history have been deeply influential on my own social-constructivist understanding of knowledge. Prominent here are Edward Hallett Carr, What Is History? (London: Macmillan, 1961); R. G. Collingwood, The Idea of History: With Lectures 1926–1928, edited and with an introduction by Jan van der Dussen (Oxford: Oxford University Press, 1994), as well as his An Autobiography, with an introduction by Stephen Toulmin (reprint; Oxford: Oxford University Press,

1978). Three German philosophers are also significant for my reflections on knowledge, language, and power: Ernst Cassirer, *The Philosophy of Symbolic Forms*, vol. 1, *Language*, trans. Ralph Manheim, with a preface and introduction by Charles W. Hendel (New Haven, CT: Yale University Press, 1953); Max Horkheimer, *Critique of Instrumental Reason: Lectures and Essays since the End of World War II*, 2nd ed., trans. Matthew J. O'Connell et al. (New York: Continuum, 1985); and Jürgen Habermas, *Knowledge and Human Interests*, 2nd ed., trans. Jeremy J. Shapiro (London: Heinemann Educational, 1978).

The feminist tradition introduced a crucial set of approaches and questions to the whole discussion of knowledge, culture, and power. Classic among the pioneering works in this area is Carol Gilligan's *In a Different Voice: Psychological Theory and Women's Development*, 2nd ed. (Cambridge, MA: Harvard University Press, 1993); Mary Field Belenky, Blythe McVicker Cinchy, Nancy Rule Goldberger, and Jill Mattuck Tarule, *Women's Ways of Knowing: The Development of Self, Voice, and Mind*, 2nd ed. (New York: Basic Books, 1997), as well Sandra Harding and Merrill B. Hintikka, eds., *Discovering Reality: Feminist Perspectives on Epistemology, Metaphysics, Methodology, and Philosophy of Science*, 2nd ed. (Dordrecht, The Netherlands: Kluwer Academic, 2003), are important, early anthologies in this respect. Patricia Hill Collins, *Black Feminist Thought: Knowledge, Consciousness, and the Politics of Empowerment*, rev. 10th anniversary ed. (London: Routledge, 2000), introduced the decisive angle of racial constructions, power dynamics, and conflicts, and their epistemological consequences. Also important from a sociological perspective are the works of Dorothy E. Smith: *The Everyday World as Problematic: A Feminist Sociology* (Milton Keynes, UK: Open University Press, 1988); *The Conceptual Practices of Power: A Feminist Sociology of Knowledge* (Boston: Northeastern University Press, 1990); *Texts, Facts, and Femininity: Exploring the Relations of Ruling* (London: Routledge, 1990); *Writing the Social: Critique, Theory, and Investigations* (Toronto: University of Toronto Press, 1999); and *Institutional Ethnography: A Sociology for People* (Walnut Creek, CA: AltaMira Press, 2005). More recently, I have been deeply impressed by the approach of Elizabeth Kamarck Minnich in her *Transforming Knowledge*, 2nd ed. (Philadelphia: Temple University Press, 2005).

Among the major Latina feminist and/or *mujerista* contributions to this conversation are Gloria E. Anzaldúa, *Borderlands/La frontera: The New Mestiza*, 2nd ed. (San Francisco: Aunt Lute Books, 1999); Cherríe L. Moraga and Gloria E. Anzaldúa, eds., *This Bridge Called My Back: Writings by Radical Women of Color*, 2nd ed. (Latham, NY: Kitchen Table: Women of Color Press, 1984); and Ada María Isasi-Díaz, *En la lucha/In the Struggle: Elaborating a Mujerista Theology*, 2nd ed. (Minneapolis: Augsburg Fortress Press, 2004).

Several Latin American and Hispanic philosophers, theologians, and other thinkers have also helped me make the connections of many of the diverse threads underlying these reflections, both among themselves and with the history, circumstances, and critical thinking emerging since the late 1960s in Latin America and among US Hispanics. Among these thinkers are Rubem Alves, with his *Filosofia da ciência: Introdução ao jogo e suas regras*, 3rd ed. (São Paulo: Editora Brasiliense, 1982), *Estórias de quem gosta de ensinar*, 2nd ed. (São Paulo: Cortez Editora-Autores Asociados, 1982), and *Conversas com quem gosta de ensinar*, 8th ed. (São Paulo: Cortez Editora-Autores Asociados, 1988); Renato Rosaldo, *Culture and Truth: The Remaking of Social Analysis*, 2nd ed. (Boston: Beacon Press, 1993); Linda Martín Alcoff and Eduardo Mendieta, eds., *Thinking from the Underside of History: Enrique Dussel's Philosophy of Liberation* (Lanham, MD: Rowman and Littlefield, 2000); Ivone Gebara, *Longing for Running Water: Ecofeminism and Liberation*, trans. David Moulineaux (Minneapolis: Augsburg Fortress Press, 1999); Dolores Delgado Bernal, C. Alejandra Elenes, Francisca E. Godínez, and Sofia Villenas, eds., *Chicana/Latina Education in Everyday Life: Feminista Perspectives on Pedagogy and Epistemology* (Albany: State University of New York Press, 2006); Orlando Espín, *The Faith of the People: Theological Reflections on Popular Catholicism* (Maryknoll, NY: Orbis Books, 1997); Orlando Espín and Miguel H. Díaz, eds., *From the Heart of Our People: Latino/a Explorations in Catholic Systematic Theology* (Maryknoll, NY: Orbis Books, 1999); Walter D. Mignolo, *Local Histories/Global Designs: Coloniality, Subaltern Knowledges, and Border Thinking* (Princeton, NJ: Princeton University Press, 2000); David T. Abalos, *Latinos in the United States: The Sacred and the Political*, 2nd ed. (Notre Dame, IN: University of Notre Dame Press, 2007); and Claudio Canaparo, *Geo-epistemology: Latin America and the Location of Knowledge* (Oxford, UK: Peter Lang, 2009).

Michel Foucault's *Power/Knowledge: Selected Interviews and Other Writings, 1972–1977*, ed. and trans. Colin Gordon (New York: Pantheon Books, 1980), is another key work for these discussions. And in my very personal case, two disparate, out-of-the-ordinary books helped me frame with a smile these issues that are all too often entangled with very real, massive human pain: Robert M. Pirsig's *Zen and the Art of Motorcycle Maintenance: An Inquiry into Values*, 25th anniv. ed. (New York: Quill, 1999), and Bernard McGrane's *The Un-TV and the 10 mph Car: Experiments in Personal Freedom and Everyday Life* (Fort Bragg, CA: Small Press, 1994).

Finally, two previous writings of mine have summarized earlier elucidations of my views in these matters: "Avertissements épistémologico-politiques pour une sociologie latino-américaine des religions," *Social Compass*

26, nos. 2–3 (1979): 179–94, and *Mapas para la fiesta*, 2nd ed. (Atlanta: Asociación para la Educación Teológica Hispana, 1999).

APPENDIX B

1. Max Weber, *Essays in Sociology*, ed. and trans. H. H. Gerth and C. Wright Mills (New York: Oxford University Press, 1946), 147.
2. Mikhail Bakhtin, *Problems of Dostoevsky's Poetics*, Theory and History of Literature (Minneapolis: University of Minnesota Press, 1984), 110.
3. Edward A. Shils and Henry A. Finch, eds., *Max Weber and the Methodology of the Social Sciences* (Glencoe, IL: Free Press, 1949), 78.
4. See James Spickard, "My Liberation Needs Yours: Ethics, Truth, and Diversity Work in Academic Life," in *Alternative Voices: A Plurality Approach for Religious Studies: Essays in Honour of Ulrich Berner*, ed. Afe Adogame, Magnus Echtler, and Oliver Freiberger (Göttingen, Germany: Vandenhoeck and Ruprecht, 2013), 320–37; James V. Spickard, "Faith, Hope, and Regulative Ideals: Epistemological Reflexivity in the Sociology of Religion," *Annual Review of the Sociology of Religion* 3 (2012): 1–23.
5. Evolutionary biologist Robert Trivers in his book *The Folly of Fools: The Logic of Deceit and Self-Deception in Human Life* (New York: Basic Books, 2011).

INDEX